the

Wisdom

of

Money

The *Wisdom* of Money

Published by SilverTree Press, a division of The Heart of Teaching, Inc. A non-profit corporation. For information address: SilverTree Press, 2240 Encinitas Blvd. Suite D548, Encinitas, CA 92024 www.silvertreepress.com

ISBN 978-0615745138

Cover design by Trevor Thomas, LightWerxMedia.com

the
Wisdom
of
Money

Listening to the Spiritual
Message of Your Finances

Alice Bandy

SilverTree Press

The *Wisdom* of Money

For Riley

The *Wisdom* of Money

ACKNOWLEDGEMENTS

This book has been a long time in the making and could not have happened without many people who inspired, encouraged and taught me along the way. Thank you to all the many wonderful teachers I have found in this lifetime: Chriss Lemmon, my teacher and friend, thank you for taking me beyond any place I thought I would ever go. Dean Brown, for showing me what it means to deeply love the human and the spirit at the same time; all of my students, clients and friends for the last twenty years at Seaside Center for Spiritual Living, Holmes Institute and across the country. I have learned more from you every day than any book could ever teach me.

I am grateful for my friends and colleagues who continue to support and inspire me: Christian Sorensen, Kathy Hearn, Linda McNamar, Roger Juline, Katherine Economou, Ross Foti, and so many others. Thank you. To my online community around the world, especially Ana and Heidi, who provided daily enthusiasm for getting it done. Thank you.

To Marianne Wilson, who offered her excellent professional know-how and inspiration for this entire project. To Trevor Thomas, of LightWerxMedia, the very talented and intuitive designer who designed the cover of this book. And Liz Ecker, for stepping in for a last minute review. Thank you

Especially to all of my friends in the Tree of Life community: your spiritual quest and love for each other is a beacon of light in my world. And most importantly to my partner, Michael Berger, who loved me and held my hand through the birthing process of this book, read and commented on every page. You remind me every day of the important things in life.

The *Wisdom* of Money

CONTENTS

The *Wisdom* of Money

INTRODUCTION

In 2008, the United States and the world economy experienced the greatest financial downturn since the Great Depression. Major financial institutions failed, unemployment reached crisis proportions and inflated housing values collapsed. The impact was felt around the world, touching millions of lives. Money became the most talked about topic in the media, at work and around kitchen tables all over the world.

During this time, I had a thriving spiritual counseling practice that grew bigger as many undertook to find answers to pressing financial challenges. Basic questions of how to survive, where to find a job, how to pay off debts, how to meet the financial needs of the family reached points of desperation.

Day after day, I talked over these worries with my clients, looked for new and deeper answers, prayed with them, visioned with them and supported them in the painful process of change. These questions and issues of money were painful to this day, and many suffer greatly from them. Horror stories of lost homes, unpaid medical bills, lost retirements swept through my office. We began to meet regularly to pick up the pieces and create new lives out of the ashes of the old.

Life is always challenging and, especially when serving as a counselor to others, I hear a lot about these rough moments. This time seemed different and more pressing. More urgent. As if money issues were rocking the very core of existence for many.

But I began to see something else happening as each person struggled with the new realities of their lives: lives without the work they had done for years, or the house they had lived in or the income they were used to having. A new level of honesty and creativity began to show itself. People who thought their lives to be settled, decisions already set, were being forced to stop and think again about the choices they had made.

The question was no longer: "How is your job going?" It was: "What kind of new job would you like?"

The question was no longer:"When do you plan to retire?"

It was: "What kind of work would you love to do to use your talents for many more years?"

A different kind of news started to pour into my office. News not usually reported in the newspapers. Stories of unemployed people deciding to become entrepreneurs and start businesses or services in fields they liked. People forced to move home or leave home or move out of state for financial reasons who reported loving the new changes. Friends helping friends to get by: babysitting for free, sharing meals, offering free services of resume writing, financial planning, and many other useful things of this kind.

My work is with the individual and so my insights into this situation were individual as well. Time after time, I sat with clients whose eyes would light up with prospect of finally doing work they loved. When they were brave enough to take the step, they were so happy. Clients who finally settled old money issues within their families out of necessity. Families who moved in together and, in close quarters, settled their differences. It was not accidental that these things happened.

It was during this time and because of these times that the tools in this book were developed. Spiritual principles are always the most powerful principles in life. Nothing in the world exists unless it is first an idea, a thought, a feeling that comes from deep within the individual. This is always true. And these inner urgings are always leading us to a better way of life. But what a pleasure it was and continues to be to watch money, the great and powerful idea of money, transform itself in the presence of truth. There is nothing in the outer world that is more powerful than the inner realities of life. This is certainly true of money.

I have been doing spiritual counseling for over 20 years and have seen the tools in this book in action time after time. But you certainly do not have to have long experience in spirituality to have them work for you. Money can be a harsh taskmaster but you can transform it into an obedient servant when you heed the spiritual principles it is showing you in your life.

The Wisdom of Money walks you step-by-step through the process of creating new levels of wealth and well being in your life. Well being. Isn't that what it is really about? We all know that, by itself, having a lot of money cannot make you happy. You are more complicated than that. You have more desires than just wealth. Each of us is seeking greater levels of health, love, freedom, joy, peace of mind, respect and personal fulfillment.

In this book, we take a deeper look. By setting a clear intention, finding your blocks to prosperity, taking time to remove them and be true to yourself, you will transform your life. Interestingly, money is an easy teacher of these things. By answering the simple sequence of questions in each chapter, you, will find that your money is teaching you not only how to be prosperous, but how to be truly happy.

It can seem that our financial community, the government, the job market, our society are running or even ruining your life. It may seem that money is just a difficult thing that brings constant worry or problems to you. This does not have to be so. You can take back your power from money worries and begin to use money as a helpful tool and a reliable guide to a happy life.

This book will show you how. So I invite you to take the journey of a lifetime with us and explore *The Wisdom of Money*. Our sights are set on levels of happiness and freedom that you may have only dreamed of before this. Open up to the natural joy and prosperity that is always here for you.

Stop being afraid and don't give up. These are the ideas and answers to create the life you would love to live. I am excited to take this journey with you. I know it will change your life. I would love to hear from you when it does.

Dr. Alice Bandy   April 2013

If you want to go deeper and join us in the online class companion with this book, you will find us at www.consciousnessofwealth.com.

The *Wisdom* of Money

HOW TO USE
THIS BOOK

Welcome to a life-changing experience of examining your money through a spiritual lens. Like everything else in the human world, money is an out-picturing of an inner belief. Everything in life begins with an idea, whether a book, a job, a relationship, or (especially) money. Before anything can have a life in this world, there first has to be a concept for it in the inner world. First the idea, then the experience follows. As you change your ideas through exercises and contemplation, as your awareness changes, your money will also change and show up for you in new ways.

This book is not an ordinary book. It requires a personal commitment to growing and changing your ideas, so that you can create a life of true joy and prosperity. The exercises included here have been proven successful with hundreds of people. They will work for you too, if you make a dedicated effort to use them for real change in your life.

To get the most from this book, make a decision to work the process through beginning to end. It is not a book to dip in and out of, since it has been planned to take you along a real inner path to success. This is a truly a workbook filled with questions and exercises that are designed to support you, step-by-step, in changing your level of prosperity. Every minute you dedicate to the process revealed here will bring you closer to the life you intend to create for yourself. Read the material, do the exercises and answer the journaling questions. After a few weeks, you will find your deepest goals for yourself and your money showing up in your life. Pay attention! Your intention sets it in motion, and your attention confirms the results. The results may begin slowly, but it is important to notice them and celebrate even the small changes as they occur. This will help your transformative process to grow rapidly.

Because this book is interactive, I recommend that you get a spiral notebook and dedicate its use to answering all the questions in these pages. You can also add into that notebook your journaling thoughts and inspirations as they come to you. Having all of your answers and ideas in one place will give you strong support in moving ahead with your intentions and goals.

As you work your way through this book, your life will begin to change. Your money will become a partner to you, a welcome addition to your creative process, a voice of reason, and a spiritual practice. As these things take place, you will discover the power of listening to your money and using its wisdom to make your deepest dreams come true. A miracle? Perhaps. Actually, it all comes from you and your natural ability to create the life you choose.

1. THE POWER OF INTENTION

Even today in our material world, there are still secrets to the universe. In the midst of our busy, heavily populated, commercial existence, there are laws of life, deeply powerful principles, working beneath the seeming surface of our day-to-day existence. This book is about those laws.

I am sitting on my patio on a beautiful, sunny day, near a big pot recently delivered to me. It holds three canes of a rose thought to be one of the world's most fragrant roses: the Paul McCartney rose. A friend found this rose and brought it to me, knowing that I loved its glorious color and fragrance. But today, on this beautiful day in January, this rose is only stalks. No leaves or flowers. My rose is sleeping, dormant in this winter season. Yet I hold a vision of this rose in my mind. I am certain that there will be a day when this plant begins to leaf out in the spring. And by summer, I know that I will have a fragrant bouquet of this wonderful rose.

Many things like this happen every day in our natural world. We are so used to it, we take it for granted. Of course the seed will sprout. Of course the chick will grow into a hen. Of course the ice will melt and the river run again. Of course the sun will rise. We know these phenomena so well. Because these are natural laws. It is just the way they work.

The wonder of life is that it creates more life. This is the very nature of life itself, to grow and expand. We see this everywhere we look. From the smallest bird to the tallest tree, the natural

Think beyond your lifetime if you want to accomplish something truly worthwhile.

Walt Disney

1

world is constantly sprouting, growing, expanding, creating more and more of itself. As a living thing, this is your nature, too: to grow and thrive. You are an amazing masterpiece of life because you are self-aware and conscious of the inner workings of your own mind and spiritual nature. You are one of the highest evolutionary species to date as a human being in this world. Your life, just like everything else, works according to the natural laws of growth that govern our planet Earth.

It is in the natural interests of all evolutionary life that you have everything you need to grow and thrive. In some ways, all of life is counting upon you to continue to evolve into the highest version of life here on Earth and to be the human being you came here to be. When you are able to be your best self, true self, you can then truly participate in life and be of service to the world. You deserve to have all that you need for a happy, healthy, creative life.

Yet often we find that this is not so. Life can seem to be a struggle. Money and resources seem hard to come by. When you are scratching to make a living, it can be challenging to have the luxury of fully expressing yourself and taking care of those you love. The great news, however, is that this kind of struggle is not necessary. Scarcity is not your natural state. Growth and expansion are your natural state. You can achieve a new way of living: one that reflects on the outside the full power of yourself on the inside.

What is This Human Life?

The experience you are having in this human world completely supports you in being yourself in all the ways you choose to be.

How is this possible? Because we live in an intelligent universe. Scientists are busy proving how smart every cell of your body is and how each one communicates with every other cell in your body to keep your systems working. Biologists can tell you about the natural world: the brilliance of how all the ecosystems work together to keep the proper levels of oxygen, nitrogen, and other essential elements in our atmosphere. Astronomers can tell you about the night sky, the life-giving radiance of the sun that makes life possible. And so much more.

The ancients used to say, "As above, so below". This wise statement describes the great intelligence of you. As all the celestial bodies of the universe correspond and harmonize, so too does your individual life harmonize with all of life. Everything in your life is here to support you in living the fullest possible expression of your true self. As the material world is vastly intelligent and conscious, even more so are you. This great life of consciousness is so vastly intelligent that we can only call it Divine, because it surpasses our understanding. Endlessly organized and realized in a variety of life forms beyond imagining in the human mind, intelligence is the substance of life itself. It is the very substance of you. It is what you are. Every cell of your body is vastly intelligent. And so is your mind. Intelligence is the essential energy of life.

We Live in a Spiritual Dimension

Whether you are aware of it or not, you are living in a spiritual dimension which sources our human life. Everything you do in your life begins with an idea in your mind that is drawn from the spiritual dimension of you.

Sometimes in the morning, I like to begin my day with a hot cup of tea. I have a favorite cup for this morning ritual that was given to me as a gift. It is a beautiful Chinese tea cup that has its own lid to keep the tea hot between sips. Although a small thing, this cup is quite wonderful, as it is covered with painted images of colored flowers and dragons and Chinese-looking birds. Sometimes when I am drinking my tea, I like to imagine the person who created this cup. How did he or she decide on the shades of the delicate flowers? Where did the winding dragon image come from? How did this unknown designer decide to curve the handle just so? This cup was created by the mind of someone very imaginative and sensitive to color and design. But there are other minds at work in my kitchen. There is the mind who dreamed up my dishwasher, or the pretty place mats on the table. Or even the wicker basket that holds my store of oranges.

Everywhere we look, we can find these examples: an idea that occurred in the mind of someone, an idea completely intangible, that created a blueprint and came into form as a material object. The creative process at work surrounds us daily. This same process takes place in every aspect of our lives. Our home reflects our inner awareness of beauty and order or lack thereof. Our bodies reflect our ideas of ourselves and whether we think enough of ourselves to comb our hair, pick out our clothes, take care of our basic hygiene. Our appearance expresses on the outside what we think of ourselves on the inside. And, our bank accounts reflect our ideas of work, wealth, security, and freedom.

The outer appearance of your life is material. But at your essence, your life is consciousness, it is intelligent life, and it is the truth of who you are. Our materialistic culture would like to persuade you otherwise. The commercial world puts up a good fight to entice you to forget that you are living your life from the inside out. It would like to persuade you that you cannot, of yourself, create your own experiences and how you live. Our material world would like to convince you that money, position and other people can make you happy. It encourages you every day to give your creative power away by identifying yourself with material things and attaching to them as necessities.

But, at the end of the day, we are smarter than this. We all know better. Deep within, we know that the long-held inner values of life—love, truth, peace, beauty, honor, joy—are really what matters most. And, when we remember this basic truth about life, we are reminded that we are spiritual beings - so much more than just bodies. We begin to sense the importance of the spiritual dimension in which we live.

What does it mean to live in a spiritual dimension? That is the fun and the mystery of life. Everything in your life is a reflection, an out-picturing of an inner dimension. It is spiritual at its source. This means it can be changed in a moment, because there is no time or space in the spiritual dimension. Time and space are part of the material world, not the inner realm of consciousness. Right now, you can think of someone you love and experience the love between you. You might imagine them far away and see his or her face. This is the power of your inner being: you can cross over the time and space between the two of you and create an experience for yourself.

I know that you have had experiences when you were able to do something that defies the usual natural laws of time and space. Perhaps you were late and in a hurry but, for some unknown reason, arrived early. Perhaps you got absorbed in doing a task and looked up to find that hours had passed, even though it seemed only minutes. Perhaps you stayed up all night celebrating a grand event in life and found you were not even

All the physical matters are composed of vibration.

Dr. Max Planck

tired the next day. Your essential self is spirit and is not bound by laws of time and space. This is the reason why some people are able to instantly heal from terminal illnesses. It is why a mother can swim across a freezing river to save her child. It is why others perform impossible feats every day. And it is why your money issues and problems can change overnight.

Vibrations of Life

Not all of life is the same. Different life forms have different energetic rates of vibration. Literally, the atoms of different life

---

Hierarchy of the Vibrations of Life:
Each level of consciousness having
dominion over the lower ones

Spiritual Plane—Superconsciousness/Awakened Intelligence
Pure Spirit
Individualized spirits
Humans of higher consciousness

Mental Plane—Conscious/ Semiconscious Intelligence
Human mind
Animal mind
Plant mind
Mineral and chemical mind

Physical Plane—Subconscious (Dormant) Intelligence
Energy so organized that it bears life characteristics
Mental phenomena, telepathy, higher forms of energy
Heat, light, magnetism, electricity
Radiant matter: radioactive waves and particles
Matter: solids, liquids, and gases

Based upon The Kybalion: A Study of Hermetic Philosophy

---

forms move at different speeds. According to their rate of vibration, they have a different density and a different nature. It is easy to see that a piece of ice has a different vibration from water. The dense stone has a different vibration from a bird flying through the sky.

The little chart on the previous page gives you a picture of how this chain of vibration operates in life. Why is this important? Notice that even the animal mind has dominion over matter, which is the lowest vibration on the physical plane. The mind of the deer can decide to flee and gives that direction to its material form—its body—and then it begins to run.

The human mind is far superior to the vibration of matter. And when the human mind rises up to states of higher consciousness, it enters the vibration of the spiritual plane. This awakens you to who you really are - an individual spirit living as a human being in a material world on earth.

This explains why certain holy men, shamans, saints, certain doctors, and others can perform what seem to be miracles in our world. They have harnessed the power of vibration to make new decisions about matter and what it will do. Just as with the fleeing deer, the mind of higher consciousness can give new direction to the material body with new results. These events seem miraculous to the average man, but they are simply a demonstration of the workings of the true nature of life. What this chart does *not* show is that, in addition to the vibrations of life having a chain of power from top to bottom, they also have a chain of power from inside out. The highest vibration of you lives at the center as the spiritual vibration and it moves outward powerfully to create the other layers of your life, eventually manifesting in your creations in the material world.

Einstein and the Quantum Mind

What does Albert Einstein know about your money? All this talk of vibration is based upon work that Einstein did in 1905. He proved that when matter is broken down into smaller and smaller parts, it eventually moves beyond the realm of matter into the realm of energy. His famous equation $E=mc^2$ proves that matter and energy are interchangeable. Energy is the basic component of all matter and of all life.

In this world of energy, nothing is static. Everything moves, everything vibrates. At the lower levels, vibration is slower, more dense. At the higher levels, the vibration is faster, lighter. The difference between the various manifestations of matter is their rate of vibration. This same idea also applies to mental, emotional and spiritual manifestations. So, for example, feelings of self-hate and grief vibrate at a very low rate; feelings of love and joy vibrate at very high rates.

There is more to this idea, however. In laboratories, scientists have attempted to create a pure vacuum, which is completely empty. This has proved to be impossible. Even a vacuum is full of energy, full of life. This and other ideas have prompted the theory of the unified field, or the theory of everything. Is it possible that all of life is connected in one web of the basic energy of life? Spiritual people have believed this for thousands of years, and now science is working to prove it.

In the famous Two Slit experiment by Thomas Young, scientists took another step along this train of thought. By attempting to explain when a single photon of light will shine as a wave or a particle, he found that the end result was decided by the mind of the observer. So, if the scientist thought it was a particle, it would be. His thought decided the result of the experiment. Since then other quantum physicists have postulated that it is consciousness itself which collapses the quantum wave of energy into the particle. In the lab, the scientist's thoughts impacted the way light was formed at the most fundamental level. This is a powerful confirmation of how the creative process works. The energy of life is conscious and receives the impress of our thought and acts upon it.

So what does this mean to you? Because of your high level of awareness, you are able to use your consciousness in the energy field of life to create a virtual template of what you intend to manifest in time and space. Clearly energized intentions must manifest on the physical plane of existence. Science has proved it. Your idea creates the vibration of matter in physical form. It is this creative process that creates your experience of life.

The Vibration of Wealth

Understanding vibration and the unified field opens up a new avenue of empowerment for you. Once you draw your attention to the process of creation, as we have just done here, you can begin to be more focused in using the process. Your silent thoughts vibrate within the field and become the seed ideas for new ways of life to be created.

At your essence, you are not material—you are spiritual consciousness, not limited by any human construct or material form. Touch in with that inner self. Feel the reality of your inner life, your inner loves, ideas, talents, passions. This is your truest self. And, joy of joys, you cannot be confined by the human or material world. Your vibration is higher than the physical realm and, as such, you have power over it. You live foremost in the realm of spirit. This inner essence of you is alive, not subject to the laws of the material universe.

Your wonderful spirit continues to grow and expand its manifestation of wisdom, its gifts, its abilities to create love, joy, and so many other beautiful spiritual qualities. Even though your physical capacities may diminish over time, your true self is eternally young and continues to grow into ever greater quality of life.

Our intention is to experience the vibration called wealth. This is a broad intention and includes the idea of wealth in the highest possible way. It means more money and resources for sure, but it also means inner wealth, well-being, peace, and joy. As you give your attention to this book, its ideas, and exercises, you are beginning to turn within the great unified field to the vibration I have named the *consciousness of wealth*.

There comes a time when the mind takes a leap to a higher plane of knowledge but can never prove how it got there. All great discoveries have involved such a leap.

Albert Einstein

9

Setting an Intention

You come into the world as a powerful spiritual being, but the experiences of the outer world can sometimes create the illusion that you are not powerful. Attitudes of others can persuade you to identify more with the human condition and vibration rather than with the inner spiritual life. Often the limited and unsatisfactory results you experience result from subconscious programming that warps your thinking. If you have issues with money or resources, there is something blocking your naturally powerful ability to create the life you want.

It does not matter what you see happening around you or what the newspapers report about the state of the economy. You deserve to thrive. You have the tools at your fingertips: your own thoughts and desires.

If you check in with your own heart, you will find deep within that this is true for you. You deserve to live and grow and live out the destiny you feel in your heart. You are unique and special and have an important role in this lifetime. Life is a blessing for you, and together we intend to realize it for you. By focusing your thought more powerfully, you can affect the unified field of life in a powerful new way. A clear intention will create a clear focus for bringing richer living to you.

So decide now to make a true commitment to living a richer life. Decide to follow this program all the way through to accomplish your goals. Working step-by-step you will find opportunities opening up before you. You will overcome the old patterns and conditioning that keeps you stuck and begin to live in a consciousness of wealth.

Locating the False Idea

So, what would it mean to you to live a richer life? How could you be more productive, happier, express more of your own unique self? In what ways can you open to an expanded view of yourself and your life so that you become the highest expression of yourself?

We begin by tracking the culprit causing your struggle. If you are not experiencing the level of prosperity that you desire, it means that somewhere in your life, something is blocking the natural creative flow of money and resources to you. On the following pages are a series of questions to answer honestly about your life and your attitudes toward money. You may have thought about these ideas before, but make a firm commitment to do the process all the way through. Even though these questions might seem potentially embarrassing or difficult to answer, it is necessary to be honest about your feelings in order to make the real progress you desire. All of these feelings and thoughts are helpful grist for the mill of processing anything that blocks your new level of freedom.

So, complete the following exercises carefully. They will pay off in ways that you cannot yet even imagine. We are engaging your truth at all levels—mental, emotional, physical, and spiritual—to support you in leading a richer life. Right now, as you begin to answer these questions, you are on your way to a higher, more powerful vibration of wealth.

Yes or No?

It is important to be able answer a yes-or-no question from your heart.

Bring your attention to your body and locate the place where you are sure of a *yes* answer. This may be in your heart or stomach, or deeper inside.

To practice, ask yourself a question for which you already know the answer is *yes*. Feel the pleasurable feeling of *yes*. Do this several times.

Now ask a serious question where you know that the answer is *no*. Feel the negative sensation of *no*.

Do this several times back and forth to feel the difference between *yes* and *no*.

Practice trusting yourself about these answers.

Questions about Money
FROM THE PHYSICAL PERSPECTIVE:

Answer the following questions as honestly as you possibly can. Allow yourself to feel and record your answers without editing them.

1. How do you feel about paying your bills? Do you enjoy it? Do you resent it? Do you put it off? Do you forget about it? What conflicting feelings do you have about this? For example, do you feel obligated and reluctant or pressured and relieved? Allow yourself to write down the many varied voices in your head that argue for their point of view about paying bills.

2. What behaviors do you find it hard to control? Are you likely to spend too much, eat too much, gamble too much, drink too much, work too many hours, worry too much? What is hard for you about these behaviors? Often negative self-judgments keep the reasons for these behaviors buried for a long time. The more open and honest you can be, the more you can root out and transform your negative ideas into a way of leading a richer life.

3. Have you gone deeply or stressfully into debt?
    Has it happened more than once?

4. Have you lost a significant part of your money or assets by unsuccessful investments? Has it happened more than once?

5. Have you lent money and ended up losing it?
    Has it happened more than once?

6. Which of the following is true for you?

True or False?

T F I think it is important to save my money in case something happens and I need it for an emergency.

T F It is important not to waste my hard-earned money.

T F Everyone should have insurance in case he or she needs it if something bad happens.

T F If you give money to other people, it sometimes comes back to you in other ways.

T F There is more than enough money to go around.

T F Rich people are less happy than middle-class people.

7. Do you hold on to stuff—clothes, furniture, appliances, papers, files, etc.,long after you have stopped using them or needing them? Is your living space cluttered with things that you never really use? What are your ideas about storing things because you possibly might want them in the future? Many of these things represent old, outdated beliefs. For example, everything that is in disarray represents something out of order in your consciousness. Your clutter reflects the clutter in your head. What is it saying to you?

Questions about Money
FROM THE MENTAL PERSPECTIVE:
Answer the following questions.

1. Do you suffer from perfectionism? Do you try to always do the perfect thing and judge yourself harshly if you don't succeed to your satisfaction?

2. How much time every day do you take for yourself? Do you keep your schedule so busy that there is little time to relax, take time off, develop meaningful friendships, etc.? How much attention and care do you devote to reducing your stress? Often our level of prosperity reflects that we do not care powerfully enough for ourselves. Do you?

3. Do you measure your success by money? When you are making more money, do you feel better about yourself? If you make less money, do you feel bad about yourself? Why? What inner beliefs about life does this judgment reflect?

4. What are your earliest childhood ideas about money?

5. What are your childhood memories of your parents' ideas about money?

6. What are your ideas about money?

7. How are your money habits like your dad's money habits?

8. How are your money habits like your mom's money habits?

9. How are your ways of handling money completely different from anyone else in your family?

Questions about Money
FROM THE EMOTIONAL PERSPECTIVE:
Answer the following questions.

1. What are your three biggest fears about having money?

2. What are your three biggest fears about not having money?

3. When you are with friends and the subject turns to money or to the present state of the economy or similar topics, do you feel

    _____fatigued?
    _____bored?
    _____worried and concerned?
    _____stimulated and excited?
    _____angry?
    _____frustrated?
    _____guilty?
    _____optimistic?
    _____loving and helpful?

4. Do you feel guilty about not paying taxes or not paying your debts?

5. When a friend of yours tells you his or her money problems, do you feel

_____fatigued?
_____bored?
_____worried and concerned?
_____stimulated and excited?
_____angry?
_____frustrated?
_____guilty?
_____optimistic?
_____loving and helpful?

6. Would you like to rob a bank if you were sure you could get away with it?

7. Have you ever wanted to make extra money at someone else's expense?

8. When you hear of people winning millions of dollars in the lottery, do you feel
_____fatigued?
_____bored?
_____stimulated and excited?
_____angry?
_____frustrated?
_____guilty?
_____optimistic?
_____sad?

Questions about Money
FROM THE SPIRITUAL PERSPECTIVE:
Answer the following questions.

1. Have you ever had your money situation seem like a clear signal of the right way to live or the right thing to do? Describe the situation.

2. Have you ever had money show up when you were trying to make a decision and you made a decision because of it? Describe the situation.

3. Have you ever donated or given money to others under difficult circumstances, just trusting that you would have enough for your needs after giving it, even though you did not know how at the time?

4. Do you feel that you can make money when you want to and give it away when you want to, and that it cooperates with you in doing so? Describe.

5. Do you feel that you have a personal relationship with your money?

6. Do you consider your money to be a useful tool for creating your life? Are there things you want to create, and do you dedicate some of your money to making these things happen?

7. Do you give money to others or invest in others so that they can fund their new creations in life? Do you view your money as a creative resource in this way?

8. Do you make financial contributions to support a charity or nonprofit organization that does work you respect? Do you use your money as a force for good in the world?

JOURNALING :
My Perspectives on Money

Reviewing my answers to the questions on *physical* perspectives, what insights and ideas occur to me when I read my answers to those questions?

What insights am I having when I read my answers to the questions on *mental* perspectives?

What insights and ideas occur to me when I read my answers to the questions on *emotional* perspectives?

What insights and ideas occur to me when I read my answers to the questions on *spiritual* perspectives?

Summary

Review all that you have written and summarize your thinking now. Try to be authentic about these statements. Write about what you think and what you believe right now. When we can see where you are now, it will be easier to move ahead.

Here is a one-sentence statement of my physical perspective on money now.

Here is a one-sentence statement of my mental perspective on money now.

Here is a one-sentence statement of my emotional perspective on money now.

Here is a one-sentence statement of my spiritual perspective on money now.

PRACTICE

Make a list of people you know and admire because of their attitudes and perspectives on money. You may include historical figures, public personalities, those you know well, or those you know only by reputation.

Name of the person	What I admire about his or her attitude toward money:

QUALITIES I ADMIRE

By reviewing the answers to the questions on the previous page, make a list of the qualities you admire in others and their attitude toward money.

1

2

3

4

5

6

7

8

How do these compare to your current statements about money?

How would your current views have to change to align with these qualities you admire?

Which of these qualities do you have already?

Setting Your Intention

It is time to begin to set your new vibration of wealth into motion. These exercises have helped to focus your ideas about money. By stating a clear intention, your clear thought begins to be a creative force in your life. It will begin to bring your intentions into your life experience through the metaphysics of the unified field of all life.

Go back to the beginning again and read all the answers to all of the questions. Read the summary you have created about your current ideas of your physical, mental, emotional, and spiritual relationship with money.

Don't be hard on yourself. Thoughts about money swirl through our culture, and so many times we live at the effect of old ideas and behaviors we don't even realize are there until we do exercises such as these. The important point now is to clarify where you are and where you want to be.

Now look again at all the qualities of the people you admire. The interesting thing is this: it is impossible for you to admire these qualities in others if you don't already have the beginnings of them in yourself. In our lives, we attract those kinds of experiences and people who are like ourselves.

We are creating our lives from the inside out. Our own feelings, ideas, and unique characteristics are attracted to these same things in others. These people you admire are reflecting to you those qualities you admire about yourself. Granted, they may not be very highly developed in you yet. However, they easily can grow when you set your intention to do so. In this way, our lives serve as a mirror for us. By looking carefully at the outside of your life, you will see the reflection of what is occurring deep within you. These are all important ideas to consider when creating new goals and intentions for yourself.

You do not admire someone who makes wise investments just because you cannot do the same. You admire the ability to invest because you too have an ability to appreciate a good investment and to make one for yourself. So, the qualities you admire in others are important in learning to understand yourself.

Consider the difference between setting an intention and accomplishing a goal. We are not setting financial goals but rather setting an intention to live in a new way. Because we are working from the inside out, our purpose here is to open up your own inner wisdom. By being clear with yourself, by standing in integrity with your own truth, you begin to gather up your personal power. You begin to create your life and all aspects of it, including money, from the rich resources within you. Your own clarity of mind and intention will produce a fundamental shift of vibration, attitude, consciousness, and empowerment about prosperity.

Think carefully about these things. Now is the time to be very focused and clear on your intention for your new relationship with the money in your life. The statement of intention on the following page will guide you in writing it out as an agreement with your inner self to live in this new way.

Remember that when you become clear about your intention, you put into the unified field a powerful new idea that cannot fail to create itself in the material world and your human experience. Choose your words carefully and infuse them with your passionate desire for a new level of experience. Never include any negatives or limiting thoughts. You are beginning to live in the consciousness of wealth today.

Focusing Your Thought

Here is a simple exercise for having greater focus and concentration.

Find a quiet spot to sit uninterrupted. Pick a single number such as the number 8 and imagine looking at it or thinking about it and nothing else. Just hold this number in your head for several minutes. Do this 3 times a day.

Alternatively, imagine a red circle and a green triangle. Imagine them side by side. Now give all your attention to just the red circle, ignoring the green triangle. Do this for several minutes.

Now switch and give your attention just to the green triangle and ignore the red circle. Do this for several minutes.

Practice this daily for greater focus.

Based upon an exercise by Dr. Piero Ferrucci in his book What We May Be

Seeds of Consciousness
ideas to plant within your mind

1. I am the highest evolutionary species on this earth. As I awaken consciously to my true spiritual nature within, I gain freedom and dominion over the mental, energetic, and physical nature in myself and my life.

2. The same creative process that occurs in all life everywhere, just as a plant emerges from a seed, is the creative process at work within me. I am living and creating my life from the inside out.

3. I am living in a spiritual dimension. My consciousness is a creative force within the energetic unified field of all life. As I focus my intention, it automatically replicates itself as a tangible form or experience in my life.

Setting My Intention

Consider this statement of intention thoughtfully, and do not base it on exaggerated need or unnecessary practicality. Rather, base it upon the qualities you admire and begin to create your new perspectives of money in your life.

Fill in the spaces below to set your intention for your new relationship with money. Remember that by writing this intention, you create a powerful new vibration in your life.

I am setting my intention here today to create a new vibration and relationship with money in my life. I am choosing to more powerfully manifest these qualities in myself:

_____

_____

_____

My intention and goal for myself and my money is to:

I set this intention powerfully and intend to bring it into my life physically, mentally, emotionally, and spiritually for the universal good of all life.

_____   _____

Signature   Date

2. ECHOS OF THE PAST

One of the interesting aspects of our human life is that although we arrive here as tiny helpless babies on the outside, we are still powerful spirits on the inside. Our experiences as children growing up are seen through little human eyes, and often we process these experiences in childish ways. By the time we reach adulthood, we have a more mature and empowered view of things, but often our old baby ideas are still echoing through us. This is almost always true about our relationship with money.

Babies and most children do not handle money themselves, but they do experience the feelings and habits of the adults around them. Parents' attitudes toward money may have been healthy and positive, or not. There is no merit in blaming your money issues on Mom and Dad when you find that you have good habits or bad habits as a result of your childhood experiences with them. In either case, the parental attitude is not your attitude. It is theirs. You can take responsibility for your own ideas and change them now if you so choose.

You must find within yourself your own ideas about money and the place it holds in your life. You are unique, individual, and walking your own path through life. The decisions you make about money and your relationship to it are important. As you approach these ideas consciously, you have all the power you need to choose your habits again and to choose wisely. Changing your life is as simple as changing your mind about

There is no way to prosperity. Prosperity is the way.

Wayne Dyer

some of these old concepts that don't work for you.

In the first chapter, we began to visit some of these old ideas and to sketch out the broad view of your emotional, mental, physical, and spiritual relationship with money.

In this chapter, you will have the opportunity to more deeply examine old ideas about money that are echoing in your mind. You now have the opportunity to keep those you agree with and to discard the rest. Because of the power of your consciousness about money, these new decisions will open a creative structure for your new life and for your new intention to come true.

My Money, My Self

Imagine a beautiful watercolor painting of an ocean. Imagine it radiant with many layers of pale blue washes that give the effect of depth to the water. If you look closely, you can almost see a light shining through the water from a reflection of the sunshine within it. The artist creates this painting by carefully applying thin layers of watery color to give the appearance of depth.

This same phenomenon is going on in your understanding of prosperity. Deep within your ideas is a light radiating your essential truth. But overlaying it are layers and layers of other colors, experiences, opinions, perceptions, that cloud and lower your vibration of wealth. Some of these conditioned ideas and experiences are positive and some are not. None of them are congruent with who you really are or your deep truth. They are not you. They obscure.your true self.

Money has no power over you except what you give it. It is time to scrape away the extra layers and reveal the truth of you at the center of your prosperity ideas and issues. It is time to claim your true power as the source of your prosperity, and to give up being subject to external conditions.

Revealing My Truth

On the following pages is an exercise that guides you through the process of identifying and isolating your own vibration of wealth. This type of exercise is more of an energetic experience than a mental process. It works with your inner being in deep ways that cannot be explained easily through a mental analysis. So, to maximize the effect of the exercise, I encourage you to turn off your mind and just go with the process. It is powerful and brings surprising results. Approach it carefully and allow enough time to do it well.

This exercise spreads over the next two pages.

On a sheet of paper or in your notebook, create three columns: one for you, one for your mom, and one for your dad. If you were raised by someone else, you can substitute his or her name in these columns.

Answer the questions that follow and write the answers in the appropriate column for each person.

If you don't know the exact answer, just answer what your general impression was at the time. Give your own answers in your own column according to how you are in your present life.

We are looking for the differences here, not the similarities,
so do not try to match your parents' answers
unless it is completely true.

Revealing My Truth

Create three vertical columns on a sheet of paper.

The first column is for you.
The second column is for Mom
The third column is for Dad.

You may substitute any other names of your early caregivers to make this exercise applicable to your situation.

Answer the questions on the following page for each person.
Place the appropriate answer in the column for each person.
Each question should be answered for each person.
See the example below.

Example: Question: How much cash did they carry at any one time?

Mom	Dad	Me
None	Few hundred dollars	$40

Questions: *Answer these questions for each person and write each answer in the person's column. See the example. If you don't know the answer, give it your best guess.*

1. How much cash did they usually carry /do you usually carry at any one time?

2. How did they make their money/you make your money?

3. How did they/do you feel about spending money for necessities, such as food?

4. How did they/do you feel about spending money for extras or vacations?

5. What did they/do you say about money? What kinds of sayings or other ideas did they/do you use to describe money (such as "money does not grow on trees")?

6. How did they/do you feel about giving money away to others?

7. How did they/do you feel about saving money?

8. How did they/do you feel about paying taxes?

9. How did they/do you feel about people who have a lot of money?

10. What was the most they every spent on one thing /you ever spent on one thing?

11. What were their/ are your spiritual beliefs about money?

12. How much of their life/your life was built according to the amount of money available?

When you have completed this list of

answers, hold the list in your hands and look carefully at each of the columns.

1. What do you notice in these columns? What are the differences in these lists? What are the similarities?

2. Look at the column that describes your own attitudes toward money. Read down the column marked "Me." Read it slowly and feel it. How does this feel to you? Close your eyes and feel these ideas in your body. Do they feel like you? Is this the person you are today—not in the past, but today? Is this the person you want to be in the future?

4. Go back over the list again and circle the attitudes that are the same for you and for one of your parents.   Are these ideas you want to keep, or do you want to change something on your list? You are completely free to change any of these old ideas that are not working in your life. Decide to be different. Use your current adult ideas to define how you live!

5. Go back to the intention you set in Chapter 1, and add any other ideas from this exercise. Make a list of the ideas you would like to change in your life.

Claiming Your Own

The exercise you just completed begins to separate out old, conditioned ideas and experiences of the past from what is really yours. Do not take it lightly. It is powerful and transformative to make these lists of differences, because your inner being renews itself through this process. You begin to find a new delineation of your own ideas and attitudes from those who have had such a big impact on your thinking.

This is a good time to take a break and give your self time to integrate this new understanding. Get up and walk around. Drink some water and come back to the book a little later. Give yourself time to fully receive the benefits of a new level of clarity. Feel the joy and relief of centering into who you are. And of what is true for you.

We are doing this exercise today on money, but it can also be done on relationships, work, hobbies, health, and/or any other area of life that you wish to explore for powerful results. Just remember to use it wisely and not to do everything at once. You are a sensitive person growing in understanding and power. Allow yourself time for the process to be easy and relaxing, rather than trying to accomplish too much at once.

Claim your own consciousness. Give up old ideas of others and feel free in your own mind. Go back and re-read your intention for your new vibration of wealth. We are under way and your intentions are working powerfully to bring your creations to you. Remember to be grateful.

Seeds of Consciousness

ideas to plant within your mind

1. I am a powerful spiritual being and I know who I am.

2. I am releasing old impressions, experiences, and ideas that I have accepted as mine, even though they belong to others. I accept only my own view of money.

3. I have the power of my own intention to create the life I choose for myself. I choose now to bring my own clear intention into manifestation in my life.

3. BREAKING OLD PATTERNS

Life is most delightful when you are free and having experiences that are true to who you are. Imagine a beautiful, highly trained horse that is the perfect specimen of health. This is a racehorse, an athlete, ready and excited to run. His mane is tossed in the wind, and his muscles ripple under his skin. He is born to run and he knows it. He will never be a pack horse and to ask him to do so is to break his spirit. He will never want to be a docile domesticated horse that small children can ride day after day. No. He is born to run and to win his race.

Think of this example when you think of yourself. You are born to live out your destiny and to win. If you try to live someone else's life or to imitate someone else's way of being, you will never succeed. Not only will you fail, you will be miserable while you do. This is one of the great underlying laws of life. You are meant to do and be what you love. You are meant to live according to your own beliefs. If you try to use anyone else's plan, you get stopped and then stuck.

Can you see the old ideas that are getting you stuck? Any time you find an idea that is matching your parents' ideas, stop and ask: is this an idea I want to keep? When you notice what you are thinking about every day, you will find that you are making your decisions and forming your attitudes about your life based upon these ideas. Once you pay attention to what you are thinking, you can start to break your old patterns of living

Money is like love; it kills slowly and painfully the one who withholds it, and enlivens the other who turns it on his fellow man.

Kahlil Gibran

and thinking about money. This takes a careful, focused approach, but you can do it. When you consciously desire change, you can make it happen.

3 Ways to Break Old Patterns

1. Consciously change the patterns around money.

Let's start at the beginning. Suppose you find that you naturally carry about the same amount of cash every day that your father used to carry. Change your pattern. Decide to carry a different amount. Do it today and every day from now on. It does not matter how much cash you carry; just carry a different amount than your father carried.

Do this for every item in the list and make all the changes you can. Obviously, you may not be able to change where you work for this exercise. But you can change how you spend your money, how you save it, how you talk about it. Make a decision to change as many things in your column as possible until your list of answers is very different from your parents.

Why does this help? Your mind and body like to work in habitual patterns, and these ideas and patterns, in turn, produce your daily life. So, if you are constantly repeating your parents' words with regard to money, your whole being starts to follow along and create the same situation with money that they had. If you want a more prosperous experience of money in your life, you will have to create it from your own, more prosperous perspective and patterns. These new ideas create a higher vibration of wealth in your life.

2. Consciously change other patterns, too.

This is the time to also change other patterns in your life. Start small. If you hold the phone with one hand all the time, begin to hold it with your other. If you get out of bed on one side in the morning, begin to get out on the other. If you always drive home a certain way, start to pick an alternate route. And so on. By changing the way you do everyday things, it is easier to expand your thinking in every area. It is easier to begin to live a new pattern of prosperity.

3. Clear the old resistance and issues.

If these exercises light up any old emotions, resentments, or angers for you, they must be cleared. We are creating a peaceful and powerful atmosphere for you to enjoy a new relationship with money and all the goodness of life. The laws of cause and effect teach us that you cannot put a negative cause into play, or allow it to persist and get a positive effect. Since you are the creator of your life, your creative energy must flow from a bright outlook and positive expectation of life.

Following are several exercises for clearing old resistance and issues. Each has a different approach, so find one that works well for you. Again, these exercises are not to be taken lightly. Set aside private moments to do them. Approach them carefully and follow all the instructions. When you are through with one, take a break and give yourself time to fully experience its effects before trying anything else. Become a student of your own reactions and processes, and allow yourself to be curious to see how you respond to these things. An open mind will carry you faster along the path of creating a new level of wealth.

Visualization for Clearing Issues

The ancient holy men used to teach about the alchemy of the spirit. Men of lesser consciousness took this idea to mean that there was a magic formula that could turn base metals into gold. Actually, spiritual alchemy creates greater value, since it transforms unconsciousness into enlightened understanding. This is a prize more precious than gold.

Today, through the power of your mind, you can experiment with both of these ideas. In this visualization, you can transmute your negative issues into a new level of prosperity for yourself. This is a fun tool, so relax and enjoy it. You may find that you want to use it regularly once you get the hang of it.

Find a quiet place where you can sit for a few moments undisturbed. Take some big, deep breaths, breathing in and releasing. Breathe consciously until you feel still and quiet on the inside. Relax and soften into your chair.

Now take one of your issues about money and bring it to mind. It may be anger at someone, fear about not having enough, old ideas, or experiences from the past. Choose just one of your issues to use to learn this exercise.

Now I would like you to imagine a beautiful golden chest. It is made of pure gold and covered with engravings that are beautiful. This golden chest is amazingly made and gorgeous to behold. And it belongs to you. You are creating its image in your mind, and it is magical in its powers.

Gently open up the lid of this golden chest, all the way open, until it is open wide.

Now I would like you to place your money issue inside of this chest. You can put in a picture of it or a symbol of it or pour the feeling of it into the chest. The chest can hold all of it, so be sure it is all inside. Then carefully close the lid so the chest can begin to work.

This golden chest will now go to work and begin to melt down your issues. Just like a blazing furnace, your chest melts down everything in it and transmutes it into liquid gold. How is this happening? Because of the amazing power of your mind.

So wait a few minutes, until you feel it is done. Then gently open the chest and see the molten gold within. This liquid gold is ready to pour into your life.

So pour. Pour it into any mold you desire: golden jewelry, a new home, a new car, a book of golden checks ready to apply to your bills, a life of deep inner joy. Pour this gold into whatever you wish for yourself.

Now pay attention. Your issue has been transformed and melted into gold and poured into your life as a new way of prosperity and joy. You have begun to create a new vibration of wealth and well-being. Pay attention to how this feels. Notice that your issue is gone, or no longer bothers you. If it comes around again, do this again.

Your thoughts are real. By the power of your thoughts, you have transmuted your issue into wealth. This visualization is part of the intention of the inner life and will eventually replicate itself in the material world.

So, once you do this exercise, give up your old ways of thinking, worry, and frustration. When these thoughts come around, place them in your golden chest and transmute them into golden images of your new levels of wisdom and wealth. Feel the freedom and joy. Keep your eye and your thought on the prize, and make the natural laws of life work for you.

Energy Exercise for Clearing

This is an exercise that gives you an energetic release of old ideas and issues. You can use it instead of the visualization, or try them both to see which works better for you. Buy some black construction paper, and buy more than you think you will need. You can use a full sheet for this exercise, or just part of the sheet. Size is not important.

Take a piece of black paper and write one of your issues on it. It does not matter if your writing is hard to read on the black paper. This is an energy exercise. So, for example, you might write:

Jealous of others who have money.

Now think about this issue and how it makes you feel. Take your pen and begin to scribble all over this black paper. Put into your scribbling all your frustrations, anger, fears, and other feelings you have about this issue. Scribble over and over until you are scribbling furiously. Scribble until you feel released, like you have no more feelings about this issue. Get all of your frustration scribbled onto the paper, until you feel empty and clear.

When you feel complete, take the piece of black paper and tear it up into very small pieces. By tearing it up, you are breaking the energy of it apart forever.

Then throw the pieces into a paper bag and take it outside of the house and throw it away. The pieces may also be burned in a safe place if you prefer. Do this with each issue.

When you are finished with an issue, go out for a walk or, even better, put on some music and dance with joy.

Spiritual Forgiveness

Forgiveness is another way of clearing issues. After all, the past is past and there is nothing to be done about it today. This day is the only day you have to live your life, so don't waste one more minute dragging the past into it.

Remember, you do not have to agree with the behaviors of the past. You do not have to think that what happened is OK or that it was right to happen. But you do have to be smart about it and to be smart about your life. If you give your power away to past events or to people from the past, or even give your power to the person you used to be, then you are condemned to repeat the past. You drag old ideas, people, and patterns with you into this bright, new moment and your potential future. Is this what you want to do?

As a spiritual being, your nature is unconditional. Even when your experiences are difficult, they do not harm the essential nature of you. You have an important destiny in this world and so it is critical to release any old energies that bind you to old lower vibrations. Carrying this old negativity from the past blocks your forward progress.

We are speaking here of spiritual forgiveness, not emotional forgiveness or even human forgiveness. Spiritual forgiveness is unemotional. It is thoughtful and powerful, but not emotional. Spiritual forgiveness is based upon the truth that you are a spiritual being. You are whole. Nothing has ever changed that. And it never will. Make this important choice for your personal happiness. Forgive, let it go, and live your life. Spiritual forgiveness will set you free.

Forgiveness Exercise for Clearing

1. Take a piece of paper and make a list of all the people in your life you have been unwilling to forgive. Be sure to include everyone you can think of, and I hope your list is long.

2. Next make a list of any money issues you are having and how you feel about them. Can you find any feelings underlying these issues? Be thoughtful and name these feelings. Are they related to anyone in your life? So, for example, if you are always short of money, do you have feelings of poor self esteem? Is there a person who treated you badly and caused you to feel bad about yourself? Find these people underlying your feelings about your money issues. Add them to the list of those who need forgiving.

3. Now, turn within and be still. Contemplate how your life would be without these old negative feelings and these people who are related to them. See and feel the freedom you might have if you release them. In your own heart, make up your mind to be rid of them. Decide to Forgive. Make a firm decision to let this old negativity go, forever.

4. Set aside enough time to go completely through your list at one sitting. Now sit quietly in your chair and bring forward the face of the first person on your list and imagine that face in front of you. Try to see them clearly, or if this is hard, create a symbol or color that represents him or her.

5. Look at him or her, or the symbol, and say:

I am sorry I gave you my power and I am taking it back now. I forgive you for putting your energy into my life, and I forgive myself for allowing it.

6. Now see or imagine the agreement you have with this person, that is so painful. This agreement can look like an old scroll, all rolled up, or a heavy burden that you carry. Imagine that you light a match to it and watch it burn to the ground. This is the end of this old, painful relationship. You can create a positive new relationship with the person if you choose, but the old one is gone.

7. Now imagine a sharp sword comes down between the two of you, cutting any old cords, agreements, bindings that connect you to the person. You are released.

8. Release the person's face from before you and call back into your own body all of your life energy that was tangled up with him or her in any way. Call back and fill yourself up with your own unique clear life force energy.

This is forgiveness. Doing it in your mind this way is just as real as doing it in person. The person is released and you are released. Forever.

Do this exercise with each person on your list. Feel the release this gives to you in your body and mind. As these old energies leave, you are free of old entanglements from the past. You are free to transform your life and your relationship with money.

Practice

After completing these release exercises, it is time to begin to create new spaces for your creative life to take place. When you are no longer weighed down with the past, you can live in new ways that bring fresh moments and bright new prospects for your future, as well as new levels of prosperity. To support yourself in this new pattern, begin the following practices.

Write down your thoughts, every morning.

No, you do not have to work through your emotional issues every morning. But you will find it helpful to download the contents of your busy mind onto paper at the start of each day.

When you arise every morning, take a few sheets of paper and write as fast as you can for fifteen minutes before you begin your day. It does not matter what you write. It only matters that you do it. Write down what you are going to do today, your grocery list, your dream fragments, your ideas about yesterday, any old angers or emotions you are still carrying. Anything at all that comes to mind. Write it down. It is not important what you write, so just let the stream of consciousness flow.

In this way, you clear a lot of space in your head every day. Try it for yourself. It helps you focus. It makes you calm. And it gives you space in your head in which to create a whole new level of well-being. What could be better than that?

Create space in your head every night.

Each night before bed, do this silly, easy exercise. Take a piece of paper and scribble your day upon it. Just make a scribble and keep scribbling until you feel that you have gotten your whole day onto the paper. Then tear it up. The day is finished. Tear it up

into small pieces and make room for a great new tomorrow.
Throw away the pieces with a little statement of thanks that you
have had the gift of living another day.

Seeds of Consciousness

ideas to plant within your mind

1. I am a powerful spiritual being and I can consciously change
   my patterns.

2. Through the power of my mind, I can transmute old painful
   issues into new levels of prosperity.

3. I live my life from the inside out. What takes place within my
   mind is a creative force for good. I set my intention to release
   old issues, and so it is.

4. I willingly release everyone in my past from any blame or
   painful experiences with me. I forgive everything, and I am
   free to move on and to create the life I choose.

4. DISCOVERING YOUR TRUTH

One of the most interesting things about money from a spiritual point of view is that once you set your intention to live a spiritual life, or at least to hold some sort of spiritual belief system as real in your life, your money conforms to your truth. What does this mean? That is the subject of this chapter: your money is reflecting your true beliefs. When you see what is happening with your money, you will find a reflection of what is going on in your heart.

We have already spent some time with how you view money through the eyes of those you admire, and we have set some goals for changing your perspective. You have also released old negative ideas and people who dragged you down and kept you from living an empowered life. Now we are taking a very important deeper look into the rest of your life and how it is reflecting your true ideas of yourself and your life. It is the beginning of a whole new relationship with your money and a new understanding of how it integrates with your spiritual life.

You are a spirit, but it is easy to forget that you are always having a spiritual experience. Your sensory perception of the material world can be so compelling and seductive that it can deceive you and make you forget who you are. Your money has a way of bringing your attention back to what you feel is important in life. We see this every day in one form or another.

What we really want to do is what we are really meant to do. When we do what we are meant to do, money comes to us, doors open for us, we feel useful, and the work we do feels like play to us.

Julia Cameron

One family sacrifices to put their child through college because they put value upon education. One man spends every cent he has on his house. One woman gives away all she has to charity. One family lives well but never gives to their church. One man enjoys a delicious lunch but refuses to tip the waiter who serves it. One family wins the lottery but loses most of it within weeks. And so on.

These examples shows us something of what each person values or does not, and where each person puts their treasure. If you keep a list of everything you spend your money on over a few months' time, you will get a clear picture of what is truly important to you in your life.

But we are going deeper. Life is deeper. We are bringing your attention to every moment of life, because moments are the basic ingredients of life. How you choose to spend your moments of time reveals how you spend your money, because they are driven by the same priorities. These choices reflect your deepest truths: the values by which you live your life.

Choices

The old story of the Garden of Eden, when Eve is persuaded to take a bite out of the apple, is an excellent story to describe what we all do almost each day.

Will we be influenced by all the cultural messages that surround us and take a bite of the apple of stress, weak habits and the opinions of others? Or will we be strong, sure, and present in the moment so that we can choose wisely how we spend our time and money?

It is so easy to zone out and not fully live our lives. So easy to turn on the TV and veg rather than paying the bills. So easy to let our belongings pile up rather than take the extra minutes to put things away or give things away. So easy to hold onto our money another week rather than paying back our friend who gave us a loan. So easy to cheat on our taxes rather than to pay our share of the costs of running our country. So easy to put something we want on the credit card rather than wait until we really have the money to pay for it. So easy to hold tight to money and refuse to assist those less fortunate than we are.

So easy at the moment, yes, but the problem is that all of these easy little choices add up to a long list of ways of living that are not in accord with the truth we believe in. Not in line with the person we want to be. And so our life and our money begin to wobble and pile up with troubles, like dirty laundry stacked up in the closet. Our friendships begin to wear out, our credit starts to slide, our bodies get soft and out of shape. One day we wake up and wonder why our life and money are not what we want them to be. Money is a blessing in this way - a wake up call to make better choices.

On the following page is a Truthful Living checklist, based upon the Integrity Checklist by Dr. Sandra Jackson, which gives you the great opportunity to take an inventory of how you are living and how to clean it up. Yes, it may seem like a lot of work if you have been letting a lot slide. But it is also a tremendous opportunity to re-create an entirely new pattern for your life based upon truth, self-care, and integrity with others. Each thing you do opens up a new, energetic pathway and open space for your abundance to flow.

Don't overwhelm yourself with this. Do one thing at a time. Just as you are forgiving others, forgive yourself for anything you find on the list. Make it right when you have the time to do it. Freedom is your great reward.

Truthful Living Checklist

Creating Space for My New Prosperity

1. Clean up my living space thoroughly.
2. Clean out my car.
3. Clean out my office.
4. Throw away or give away thing I don't want.
5. Return anything I have borrowed.
6. Organize my files and records.

Restore Integrity to My Relationships

1. Acknowledge any broken promises.
2. Correct any lies I have told.
3. Bring into the open anything secret or hidden.
4. Make amends or apologize where needed.
5. Forgive where necessary.
6. Communicate anything that must be said.

Bring Integrity to My Finances

1. Make arrangements to pay any debts.
2. Collect any money owed to me.
3. Pay my bills on a timely basis.
4. Organize my finances.
5. Pay any overdue taxes.
6. Make a plan for what I will spend, what I will save, and what I will give each month. Be sure to include giving to myself and to organizations important to me.

Create Balance for My Own Being

1. Consider my health. Am I eating a healthy, balanced diet that makes me feel good and brings me well-being?
2. Am I exercising in ways that benefit me and support my physical body to function well?
3. Do I take time for myself each day, to meditate, contemplate, dream, and commune with myself? Do I have a spiritual practice that puts me in touch with the true meaning of my life as a spirit?
4. Do I take time to play and enjoy life?
5. Do I take time to love and say "I love you" to those important to me?
6. Do I take time to appreciate those in my life who help me every day? Do I remember to say "thank you"?
7. Do I spend time in nature often to learn her lessons?
8. Do I remember to be grateful every day for my life?

Bring Truthfulness to My Time

1. Consider if the work I am doing is my true work.
2. List my daily activities. Where am I wasting time?
3. Decide to give a portion of each day to activities that are important to me and bring meaning to my life. Begin to do this daily.

Be Centered in My True Self

1. Remember that I am a spirit living also as a human being.
2. Remember that my heart knows the truth. Do I listen to it?
3. Realize that I am walking in a spiritual world as well as a material world. Do I listen and learn from my own experiences so that I can grow and be my best self?

Speaking the Truth

One of the great challenges of being human is that we live here together with so many who have differing opinions, attitudes, personalities, behaviors, relationships, and perspectives.

On one hand, this great diversity of people is a wonderful thing and adds to the rich fabric of our lives. All of these unique individuals mirror back to us the magnificent expanse of the spiritual life we are leading. On the other hand, these other individuals press upon us and sometimes make it difficult to be who we are. Instead, of being confident in ourselves we may find that we are bending, compromising, and imitating, or saying what we think someone wants to hear.

This often starts in childhood with an effort to please our parents, and it continues into adulthood. Little by little we may find ourselves not speaking what we truly feel or think. Eventually we can lose ourselves in the great human soup of thought and the emotions of our culture. We become more interested in fitting in with the rest than being who we truly are.

For thousands of years, spiritual teachers and mystery schools have taught the first principle of spiritual living: *know thyself.* The great essential corollary to this principle is: *be true to thyself.* Until we begin to say and live what is in our hearts and minds, we are leading false lives. This is a source of suffering and alienation for many, many people. It is also one of the main reasons for money issues.

I once worked with a young woman who was completely overrun with her parents ideas about life. Although she was twenty-five and living on her own, she could not hold a steady job. Everyday she woke up filled with fear that her life was slipping away from her. She was enormously depressed. She was dragging herself through the day, doing work she hated, barely existing. It took time, but gradually we worked on ideas of truth. We separated out her tastes from her family's tastes, just as you did in Chapter 3. She decided to quit the job she hated and went back to school to learn more in a field she enjoyed. Little by little, she began to speak the truth for herself to those around her. Over time, she found work that she loved, a man she loved, a new level of prosperous living and most importantly, a new love for herself. By living according to her own truth, she created a genuine life that she truly wanted to live.

It is easy to be so mesmerized by the outer world or so influenced by others that we forget how life really works. Fortunately, science has begun to explain it in ways that spiritual people have known for thousands of years. At the base of our life, we are all connected. We are all part of the unified field of life. So, when we are not being exactly who we are, it affects everything. When we are not giving our true talents, our natural rewards cannot find us. When we are not speaking our own truth, our true ideas cannot be the creative force in our lives that they are designed to be. If we come from a false cause, a false effect is the result. We are using the basic creative process of life against ourselves.

These things are pretty abstract until you try them out and see that they are true in your own life. So, I suggest that you begin now to harness the miracle of truth. Start today and make a decision to do only what you love and to only speak the truth. Remember, this means to only speak for yourself from your heart. Not to criticize or be negative with others. This next exercise will support you in reawakening your abilities to speak the truth. As you practice it, your life begins to reawaken in ways that restore the richness and joy to all that you do.

The Consciousness of Truth

Often, we feel the pressures of others so strongly—their opinions, their ways of living, their objections. Or perhaps it is the culture: the TV commentators, the media, people we admire. It becomes difficult to find our own truth. Our heart becomes flooded with the ways we should feel, instead of the ways we actually feel. The next exercise will start you on the path of reclaiming your truth. It can take a long time to learn to courageously live your truth. Be patient with the process.

Part 1

The following is a list of popular topics in the world today. Read the statement and then answer the questions below. **Remember that your brain, your heart, and your spirit often have different perspectives!**

1. Global warming threatens our ability to live on this planet.

What does our culture tell you about this?

What does your brain tell you about this?

What does your heart tell you about this? Turn inside and ask your heart what it has to say. This can be feelings, a sensation, or actual words.

What does your spirit tell you about this? Go within and open yourself up to any inner guidance there for you on this subject.

What do you choose to think is true for you about this now?

2.   **A loving, intimate relationship with a spouse or partner is challenging, and very few people are successful at it.**

What does our culture tell you about this?

What does your brain tell you about this?

What does your heart tell you about this? Turn inside and ask your heart what it has to say. This can be feelings, a sensation, or actual words.

What does your spirit tell you about this? Go within and open yourself up to any inner guidance there for you on this subject.

What do you choose to think is true for you about this?

3. **Money is a reward for hard work. If you don't have
    enough money, you are not working hard enough.**

What does our culture tell you about this?

What does your brain tell you about this?

What does your heart tell you about this? Turn inside and ask
your heart what it has to say. This can be feelings, a sensation, or
actual words.

What does your spirit tell you about this? Go within and open
yourself up to any inner guidance there for you on this subject.

What do you choose to think is true for you about this?

4. **Most people cannot make a living in jobs that fulfill their life purpose.**

What does our culture tell you about this?

What does your brain tell you about this?

What does your heart tell you about this? Turn inside and ask your heart what it has to say. This can be feelings, a sensation, or actual words.

What does your spirit tell you about this? Go within and open to any inner guidance there for you on this subject.

What do you choose to think is true for you about this?

Now go back and review the final statements of each of these pages. Make a list below of the answer to each of the last questions: what you believe is true.

What I choose to believe is true:

1. Here is what I choose to believe is true about global warming

2. Here is what I choose to believe is true about an intimate relationship

3. Here is what I choose to believe is true about money

4. Here is what I choose to believe is true about meaningful work

Two things are happening during this exercise. On one hand, you have taken the opportunity to make true statements of your own beliefs. On the other hand, you are able to more closely see examples of these things being true in your life.

Read back over these statements and make sure they represent what you actually think about these topics. It does not matter whether your statements are negative or positive. It only matters that you feel they are true for you. Are they true?

Read these statements again. As you read them to yourself, say to yourself: this is what I believe is true. Do this several times and notice how you feel as you speak the truth for yourself.

Look at your life. Can you find examples in your life that prove that these statements are true?

Practice

Make yourself a book of your truths. Use several sheets of paper to do this, or perhaps buy yourself a pretty notebook for this purpose.

Every morning when you arise, make a list of what is true for you that morning. It can include your feelings, ideas, thoughts, expectations—anything. Just a list of what you know is true *for you* **today**. The only rule about this is that it has to be true *for you only*, not for anyone else.

Every night, do the same exercise. Make a list of what is true for you on this night, after living this day of life. Continue this exercise every day.

Seeds of Consciousness

ideas to plant within your mind

1. It is completely my choice how I live my life.

2. I receive information about everything in life from our culture, from my own mind, my own heart, and my own spirit. I alone decide what I wish to believe to be true.

3. I am free to believe what I choose to believe in all areas of life. I am willing to live my life according to my own truth.

4. When I speak for myself and speak what is true for me, I create for myself a life and way of life that reflects the truth of who I am.

5. YOUR DEEPEST DREAM

A man goes to sleep in the town
where he has always lived, and he dreams he's living
in another town.
In the dream, he doesn't remember
he's sleeping in his bed. He believes
the reality of the dream town.
The world is that kind of sleep.
The dust of many crumbled cities
settles over us like a forgetful doze,
but we are older than those cities. We began
as a mineral. We emerged into plant life
and into the animal state, and then into being human,
and always we have forgotten our former states,
except in early spring when we slightly recall
being green again.
That's how a young person turns
toward a teacher. That's how a baby leans
toward the breast, without knowing the secret
of its desire, yet turning instinctively.
Humankind is being led along an evolving course,
through this migration of intelligences,
and though we seem to be sleeping,
there is an inner wakefulness
that directs the dream,
and that will eventually startle us back
to the truth of who we are.

From *The Essential Rumi*
by Coleman Barks

Know Thyself

As we touch the truth of ourselves, we begin to touch the deeper truth of the spirit we truly are. The closer we come to the truth of who we are, the closer we harmonize with the essence of our own individual spirit, and the more our life balances. It is a principle of life that the more true you are to yourself in all the choices you make, the more your life reflects those choices. You become more satisfied with your life and with yourself. Often it seems that you gather speed and power in moving toward your goals. You tap into a power of truth that is larger than you are, and you find that you can create and live in ways you have only imagined before this moment. This is the power of truth.

When your heart is open to your own truth, you will also find that you are able to say things to others that you might not have been able to say before. It is as if there is an unspoken agreement among all of us to take a truthful person more seriously. We recognize the truth when we hear it. So, as you begin to speak for yourself, remember the power of truth may be greater than you are used to having. Remember to be kind and compassionate with the views of others. Speak the truth for yourself. What is true for you? We do not all share the same views because we are each unique and individual. We cannot speak for each other. Speak for yourself. When you come from this honest place, you can speak gently and be heard.

By living in truth, we are drawing closer to the core. Closer to the dream of our life that we carry inside. As the sixth-century poet Rumi said:

> *What was said to the rose to cause it to open*
> *was said to me here, in my chest.*

As you walk in truth, let your heart open and allow the deepest dream to grow and bloom.

The ancient mystery schools of Greece used to have one sign that hung over the doors of their meeting rooms, and it said *Know Thyself.* These words have been mistakenly associated with the self-help generation, therapy, and new-age indulgences. In fact, the words *Know Thyself* are perhaps the most powerful spiritual guidance anyone could ever want or need. By truly becoming aware of yourself as a spiritual being and embracing more deeply your divine nature, you have a true basis for understanding everything. You can see your life as a microcosm of the great macrocosm of all life. You begin to understand that your life is a reflection of the all-intelligent, Spirit that is the essence of life. Now we are drawing closer to that essential you and the great Divine dream at the center.

Starting Here, Starting Now

It does not really matter where you begin. It only matters that you do begin. In some way, the amount of money you have in your life right now is helping your deepest dream to manifest itself in your life. This is always true. So, if it is hard for you to see this operating in your life, spend a little more time with the idea. Or ask a spiritual friend to talk it over with you.

We each carry within us an idea of ourselves. Our lives follow along with us and match our ideas. Of course, we can change our ideas, and then our lives change.

Think of all the times you have seen this principle operating in someone else's life. Look at the women who lose weight to make themselves more attractive, then start to think of themselves as attractive, and then attract love into their lives. Think of the men who go "middle age crazy" and begin to drive sports cars and date younger women to live a younger way of life. Think of the at-risk teens who get into an after- school sports programs, begin to be good at a sport, and start to feel better about themselves. They often go on to succeed in their lives because they have a new idea of themselves. Think of any professional athlete or Olympic champion who supercharges and focuses his or her thinking to carry himself or herself through to the win. And on and on. There are endless examples of this. And you are one of them.

So, take a few moments to answer the following questions:

1. How does my current level of prosperity reflect my ideas of myself? How does it reflect my low self-esteem or my own pride in myself?

2. How does the current level of my prosperity push or pull me into doing things that draw me closer to my dream of my life? What do I do because of my level of prosperity that draws me toward my dream?

   If you cannot see this at work in your life, spend some time contemplating this idea. Ask your heart to explain it to you. Or ask a spiritual friend to help you answer this question.

3. What am I doing now that I would not be doing if I had more money? How is the fact that I am doing this draw me closer to my dream of my life?

Fill out the chart below to visualize the role money is playing in creating your dream. Remember, even the negatives point you toward making changes that create a more positive life.

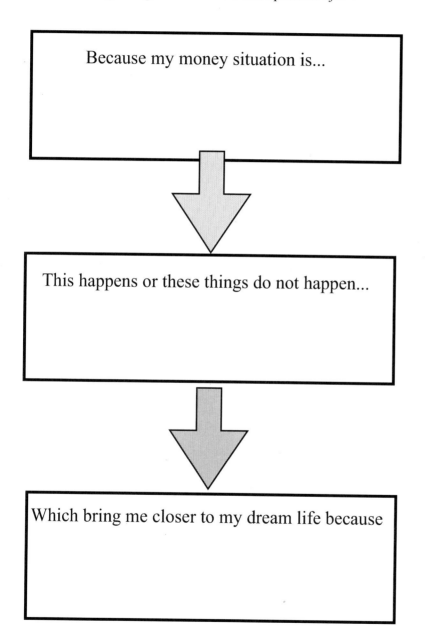

Because my money situation is...

This happens or these things do not happen...

Which bring me closer to my dream life because

I encourage you to go over and over this exercise until you can see every small way that your money or lack of it is impacting your life.

Like everything else, your money situation is one more way of finding your way to your deepest dream. We can often see the role that other people play in our lives, or the role that our health plays in life. But money is equally powerful. Because money is precious in our material world, it has a powerful energy to motivate you, reward you, make you feel worthy or unworthy. Lack of money can drive you into a deeper faith. It can make you creative and push you to change jobs, start a new business, create more streams of income, pay back debts, ask for loans, give loans, create new relationships, and hundreds of other things.

What do you do because of your money? Or because of your lack of it?

Journaling Summary

Review this chapter and look at your work. We have walked through the ways that money or lack of money are pushing you toward your deepest dream. How is this true for you?

We have looked at all the choices you have for the levels of prosperity you experience. Why is your current choice the right one for you right now? Even though you may not like it, how does it perfectly reflect your present state of mind?

The final question is: what does your money have to say to you about the great Divine dream of your life? That is the topic we will address next.

Seeds of Consciousness

ideas to plant within your mind

1. The most important task of my life is to *know myself.* By knowing myself, I am able to align with my own truth and live the life I came here to live.

2. Just as with everything else in my life, my levels of prosperity are a reflection of my idea of myself.

3. I know who I am. I am willing to learn. As I know myself better, my vibration of prosperity rises.

4. I hold the power to create the life of my dreams.

6. THE DIVINE VOICE OF MONEY

Yesterday, I woke to find storm clouds gathering outside of my window, threatening rain. Since I was going out, I went to my closet to find my little travel umbrella and put it by the door so I would not forget it when I left. When I went to shower, I found that it took a little while for the water to heat up, so while I was waiting, I stuck a few hot rollers in my hair. After showering, I remembered that I had not picked up my blue sweater at the cleaners, so I decided to wear the green one instead. When I went to the kitchen, I realized that I would be gone for many hours, so I ate a high-protein breakfast that would last. Finally, checking the time, I left ten minutes early so that I could get gas in the car on the way.

Just a routine day, you might say. Nothing special. But notice how I made all of these decisions. Easily moving in the flow of my day, making choices according to the situation before me. Planning the easiest possible way. Not resisting my choices, moving with the flow of circumstance.

Why don't we do this with money? Every week I hear of people complaining about their money. "I don't have enough money to take the trip and I really need a vacation." or "I have to take the class to complete my program, but I can't afford it." or "I want to go shopping for a new car, but I can't afford it." Or, the ever popular, "I don't have a lot of money. What is wrong with me?"

Somehow money has this huge energy that twists us inside out. To go back to the previous example, you will notice that when it looked like rain, I did not stop to question my own value as a person if I had to take an umbrella. When the hot water was not there immediately, I did not cry with impatience over the wait. I used the time to style my hair. When my blue sweater was not available, I wore something else. For breakfast and getting gas for the car, I planned ahead. I did not become angry about having to take care of myself. We all do these small things every day without judgment or negative feelings. Why don't we do the same with money?

If our money supply contracts, why don't we just work around it? If we don't have enough for what we want to do right now, why do we get so upset instead of just finding another way? Why don't we plan ahead and take care of ourselves as easily as we do when we have to go on an outing in the rain?

Because our culture places so much importance upon money, we make it more important than it is. The cold reality is that we cannot take it with us when we die, it cannot make us happy, and it does not define the truth of us. And, if you have ever spent time at the lower levels of prosperity, which most of us have, then you know it is possible to do and create many, many things in this world without money. All the things we most value: love, happiness, joy, freedom, well being, cannot be had for a purchase price. This means that despite all the drama around money, it is not necessary for most of the important things in life. Desirable perhaps, but not necessary.

Still, we have many day-to day-needs for money. Food, clothing, housing, and many of the things we love about life cost money. So, don't misunderstand me. I am not suggesting that you live without money. Quite the contrary. I am suggesting that you develop a more realistic, down-to-earth, everyday relationship with money. Just like everything else in your life, money ebbs and flows. You can learn to manage your money from the inside. You can learn to cooperate with it, to use it as a tool, to create it when you want it. And if for some reason you don't have enough money, you can transform your ideas about money so that it never prevents you from fulfilling your life. You are able to adjust to the flow of money more easily when you begin to listen to its divine voice.

Listening to Your Money

The great holy men and saints who have walked this earth sometimes speak of the great hum of the universe, the sound of life itself. Many of us meditate and learn to listen to what we know as the "still small voice within." This is our own silent knowing, our intuition, if you wish, our own spiritual guidance. Those who love nature and spend a lot of time out of doors become accustomed to the call of the hawk, the quickening of the wind, the song of the bird, the yowl of the bobcat, the soft step of the deer. All of these sounds are part of our earthly experience, part of our world.

But there is a deeper listening that must take place if you are truly going to understand who you really are and why you are here. You are a spiritual being, an expression of the spirit of life itself. You live in a spiritual universe. You are surrounded by a material universe, but even the most dense matter of our world is found to be energy, particles of light, at its center. You are walking a spiritual path of growth and expansion every day.

And the best part is that all of life is cooperating with you to do exactly that. Does it make sense? Is your life really supporting you in living out your own destiny? It cannot be two ways. This is either a spiritual experience you are living or not. It cannot be only a material existence for you.

You are more than that. You are a complex creature filled with ideas, emotions, dreams, and imagination. You have the ability to take an idea out of your head and use your hands to bring it into form on this earth. You are endless, infinite, and spiritual. All aspects of you: body, heart, mind, and soul, live here powerfully together in this human world.

This is the great excitement, the great challenge of your human life. The good news is that everyone and everything is cooperating with you. Have you ever noticed that when you are feeling low, everything seems to go wrong? When you feel bad about yourself, others around you seem to agree with you about it? When you are angry, everyone seems to want to argue and fight? When you are tired, everyone seems to want something more from you? And, when you are happy, even the weather seems to cooperate? Have you ever noticed? If not, it is time to pay attention. Begin to journal every day about how your life around you cooperates with your feelings and ideas.

Whether you are positive or negative, you will find that you attract others who encourage you to go and act more in the direction you are already going. You are in the driver's seat of your life, and everyone else cooperates with you. These are subtle ideas and it is necessary to pay close attention to their workings in action. A lot of this is unconscious behavior, but that does not make it any less true.

Your money is the same. It cooperates with you and your ideas and feelings about yourself. It encourages you along the path you are already going. It is not a measure of you or of your value. If you pay close attention, you will find that this is true.

Let's take an example. If you have low self-esteem, money **does** match your ideas about yourself. It does **not** reflect that you don't deserve wealth. What it does do is this: it encourages you along the path you are already going. So, if you have no money *and* you believe that money is a measure of your value, then you can use the fact of having no money to continue to have low self-esteem. **Your money reinforces the ideas you already have.** On the other hand, it is possible to have low self-esteem and have a lot of money if you do not use money to measure your value.

If you believe that life is hard and you must work hard to get by, then you will always work hard for your money. Your money will prove you to be right.

You are valuable, beyond any human measure. Even though it is common in our world for people to sell their time and talents, and maybe even their lives, for money, this is all false. It is a misguided sense of values that makes it this way. If you have money or don't have money, it does not change who you are or your value. Your true value is always the same: priceless.

So let's put to rest the idea that you don't have the money you want because of low self-esteem. The truth is: if you have low self-esteem, you probably don't have a lot of things. You probably don't have the relationship you want, the health you want, the friends you want, the sense of joy you want. And, of course, the level of prosperity you want. Self-esteem is just one example of how your entire life reflects your feelings, your angers, your fears, your ideas about yourself and about life.

Money to the Rescue

The good news is that money is so obvious, so conspicuously present or absent, that it is a very convenient tool for you to use to move ahead and improve the way you live. This happens when you listen to its voice in your life. You will not necessarily be free when you have a lot of money. However, you can choose to have a lot of money when you are free.

So, now is the time to begin to listen to the voice of your money. It does not lie or trick you or mislead you. Like everything else in your life, it is here to cooperate with you in finding your way, building your dreams, and expressing your own spiritual talents and truths in the easiest possible way.

The Voice of Your Money

How do you listen to the voice of your money? Here are some examples to give you an idea. But remember, you must listen carefully to yourself. Only you know what runs deep inside of you. You must begin there, at the inside, and be true to yourself. Listen from within to the voice of your money.

EXAMPLE NUMBER 1

You want to take a night class, but it is expensive and you do not have enough money to do it. "Enough" means that your money is accounted for in other ways and you do not feel comfortable paying for the class with the resources you now have. Your money is talking to you. What is it saying?

First, consider any other avenue you might have for obtaining the money for the class.

a) You might borrow it from your friend, but you just had an argument with him and don't want to ask him.

b) You might put it on your credit card, but you feel that you do not want to carry the debt.

c) You might negotiate with the teacher to pay over time for the class. This feels embarrassing and you do not want to ask for special favors.

Given all of these examples, your money may be saying one or more of these possibilities:

a) Make up with your friend and remember that you are here to be a source of love and not conflict with others.

b) Perhaps you could look at your future and see it in a more positive light so that paying off the credit card will be easily done. Or, possibly, it would be good to look at your actual spending on the card and concentrate your resources on your priorities rather than on careless spending.

c) Possibly it is time to honor yourself and the opportunity to take the class by negotiating in your favor in a way that allows you to pay over time without straining your resources. Are you respecting your own needs and treating yourself with kindness? Will this class assist you in growing your own self-respect and self-worth?

d) How are you living your dreams and ambitions? Are you feeling positive about your future and knowing that you are secure and safe, no matter what happens?

Do you see the possibilities here? There are these and many, many more possibilities to examine when listening to the message of your money. You may resonate with more than one of these. There may be other underlying issues to resolve. Or, finally, it may just be that it is not in your highest interest to take this class right now, so there is no money to do it now.

When you listen deeply to the voice of your money, you will find your answer.

EXAMPLE NUMBER 2

It is the first of the month, and you do not have enough money in your checking account for your mortgage or rent payment.

First, consider any possible avenues you may have for obtaining the money.

a) You could dip into your savings or reserve account, but it scares you to pay for living expenses out of savings.

b) You could call your bank or landlord and arrange for late payment. You hate this option because it could hurt your credit or your reputation.

c) You could take on extra work to make up the difference, but you are tired and feel that you have been spending too many hours working as it is.

d) You could call your sister and ask her to pay back the money you loaned her a few months ago, but don't want to hassle with her about it.

e) You could find a cheaper place to live that is easier to afford, but you really love where you live.

f) You could just not pay it and see what happens. Some of your friends are doing this, so why not? But it does not seem like an honest choice to you.

Given all of these examples, your money could be saying one or more of these things

a) It is time to set some goals and to examine your values for how you handle your money. Are you getting paid what you are worth? Do you spend your money in ways that bring real value to your life? Do you have confidence in yourself to create a strong, secure future for yourself? Do you know that life is on your side?

b) Are you forgiving of yourself when you experience the twists and turns of life? Are you willing to speak up and ask for special treatment when necessary? Do you feel that you are a priceless being whom others enjoy assisting?

c) Do you love your work? Does it express who you are? Is your life balanced? Are you using your creativity in the most productive ways?

d) Do you support your sister by recognizing her own greatness and power? Do you see her as successful and able to repay her loan because her life is also an expression of her own powerful spirit?

e) Do you love yourself enough to provide a wonderful home for yourself?

f) Are you in integrity with your money in all aspects of your life?

Do you see the possibilities here? There are these and many more possibilities to examine when listening to your money. Or there may be other underlying issues to resolve. When you listen deeply to your money, the answer will be there.

EXAMPLE NUMBER 3

This example has to do with a common belief that many people have that someone else is getting in the way of your money. There may be endless ways this happens and it is important for you to look at the unique circumstances of your life to see if this is so. But, for the sake of our process here, I will give a few examples of ways this could happens.

You are working at your job and putting in a lot of hours, giving great value for your time, and feel that you deserve acknowledgment for all of your accomplishments. When you come up for review, however, there is no raise for you. And you are asked to work harder for the same money.
Or...
You are a salesperson exceeding your quota month after month. With your great work ethic, you organize a team of people to go after one big account together, in order to give the client the best possible service. When the account is won, the commission is given to someone else.
Or...
You have been working hard, earning good money for a while. When it comes time to take a vacation, you want to spend some money for a very nice getaway. Your partner or spouse refuses to go since the economy is poor, and he or she says it would be better to save the money and stay home instead.

Do you get the picture? In all of these examples, someone else is standing in the way of your money coming to you, or your freedom to spend it.

Your money is talking to you. What is it saying?

Possible messages to you from your money:

a) You are carrying an old resentment about someone in your past and it keeps showing up in these kinds of situations, blocking your natural prosperity. Who is it? Who do you believe has treated you unfairly? Is it an old childhood grievance about a parent? It is time to clear it now.

b) You have an ongoing idea that you are not appreciated for who you are and all that you are able to do. Where does this idea come from? It is time to visit the earliest incident that caused you to create this idea and clear it.

c) You are unwilling to forgive the incident of your past and the people in it. Until you do, your resentment, anger and lack of forgiveness prevents your money from coming to you. Can you forgive the past? It is time to do it now.

d) You feel that you are a powerless person, and this includes being powerless about your money. Why do you feel this way? Is it true? Ask your heart for guidance about this idea.

Your money is talking to you, giving you new examples so that you can see where you are carrying old resentments and invalidations into your present experience. These old ideas need resolution now.

Universal Good

There is one more critical ingredient to consider before we go further, and that is the concept of universal good. What would it mean for something to be for the universal good? What do you think? So much of this depends upon your own ideas about life. From the spiritual perspective, anything that is for the universal good has to be good in all ways. This means that it harms no one and that everyone benefits from it. It is universally good for everyone. To take it one step further, not only is it good for all, but, in its very best form, it actually improves life for mankind. It adds to the greater and greater good of life for everyone.

When you align your personal goals with the universal good, you can harness the enormous power of the unified field. It is not just your single thought creating in the unified field. It is the collective idea, the universal energy, creating powerfully and profoundly. When you align your personal goals with the universal good of all life, it lifts you to a higher vibration and greatly increases your ability to create.

So, you need to ask yourself: why would your having money be something that is contributing to the universal good? Let's look deeply at that question.

To begin, let's look deeply at you. You are an expression of the spirit of life. You hold within you enormous talent, ideas, insights, imagination, intuition, love, and many more divine qualities. You are here to make a true contribution to our world, a contribution only you can make. The fact that you are here is important to all because no one can make your contribution for you. Only you can do it. Your presence here is universally good for all of us.

Here are some more potential answers to the question of why your having money contributes to the universal good:

1. If you must clear old issues, hatreds, angers with others in order for your money to flow to you, you bring greater peace to your life and to ours.

2. If you must improve your self-respect and begin to live a life that is more honoring to who you are and all you have to give in order to have money, this is for the universal good because you become a full participant in life.

3. If you move into work and lifestyles that allow you to contribute your talents in a more free and full expression to our world, all of us will benefit from your gifts.

4. When you realize that your dream life and the universal good are one, you begin to harness the full power of life to put your dream into motion. It does not matter how small or large your dream may be. It is for the universal good.

The great magic of money is that it asks all of these questions of you. It does not let you sit still. It is a great energy for creativity and change. And when you are living a consciously spiritual life, it demands that you examine your motivations and talents to align your goals with the universal good.

Practice

1. Spend a few minutes contemplating your money from the examples given here. What is your money saying to you?

2. How does your intention for yourself in this life line up with the universal good? If you were able to achieve all that you wish, to have all the money that you would like to have, how would all of us benefit from your fullest expression of your life?

Listening to Your Money

In the next chapter, we will begin to clear some of these old patterns and open up to the Divine voice of your money speaking to you in ways that not only improve your circumstances, but open you to the subtle joys of your spiritual path. This may seem like a miracle to you, but, in fact, it is the sort of magical way that life truly works.

For now, it is important to give careful attention to the voice of your money so that you fully gain the deep understandings it is offering to you.

I encourage you to devote a few days to journaling the answers to the questions on the following pages before continuing the process. This prepares the way for you to take courageous steps into a bright new level of understanding, prosperity, and joy.

Journaling

Answer these questions each morning for 4 days.

What is the condition of my money today? Is it plentiful, borrowed, loaned out, missing, lacking, accounted for, supporting my well being, in full integrity with my values, or...?

What is my money making it possible for me to do today?

What is my money making it impossible for me to do today?

What do I think in my mind that my money is telling me today?

What do I feel in my heart that my money is telling me today?

What is my spiritual understanding about this today?

7. THE COURAGEOUS HEART

What would it take for you to be courageous? Stop and consider for a moment what you are willing to do to have the life and lifestyle that you truly desire. Are you willing to transform old patterns of thinking? Are you willing to give up old ideas that you have held for a long time? Are you willing to change behaviors of a lifetime? Are you willing to let go of friends, jobs, relationships, situations that bind you to the past?

You might think so. But consider carefully: are you ready for real change? When you decide to embrace real change, it is not always fun. It means that your life will not be the way it has always been. It means that you might be uncomfortable for a while until you get good at new ways of doing things.

It means you might be afraid for a while until you really get your new muscles of faith and courage built up. It means that you might have to be honest in all that you say and do. Your body might be uncomfortable with this much change and try to persuade you that change is not good for you or will make you sick. Your friends and those you love might be uncomfortable with this much change and try to persuade you that you are just fine the way you have always been. You might encounter new problems of how to manage more money, how to spend it or how to save it, on a level you have never had to deal with before. And the whole thing might seem like more work and

A wise man should have money in his head, but not in his heart.

Jonathan Swift

87

more turmoil than you want to have in your life.

So, if you are not willing now to do what it takes to make this kind of step, I suggest you spend the necessary time working with this book until you are ready. Take your time and be patient with yourself. It is OK to go slowly. There is no rush. A long, eternal life stretches out ahead of you. Plenty of time to have all kinds of experiences as you progress along your spiritual path. You can move gradually ahead at a pace that does not scare you, knowing that eventually your dream will arrive.

On the other hand, I can promise you that if you are willing to have a courageous heart, if you are willing to put up with all that I have listed here and more, you can move quickly into a new life that can be described as miraculous. You will heal your relationship with money and accept it as the gift that it is. You will come into harmony with your own being, your own truth, and the lives of those you choose to love. You will feel that you have come home to your real self, perhaps for the very first time.

Taking Small Risks

As you go through the process, it is important to bring your attention to the new life, the new version of yourself, that you are creating. Now is the time to take some small risks in your life. I don't mean things that endanger you or someone else. I mean something you want to do but have been afraid to try. Say something you really mean for the first time. Try a new hobby or sport or public speaking—something you have never done. This is the way to develop courage and to move into a period of change, a new level of wealth. Even better, make a game of your life and see how many small risks, how many small changes, you are willing to make every day.

One summer evening, I was invited to participate in a fire walk. We drove to the top of a mountain where an enormous oak wood fire was burning, perhaps six feet high and seven feet long.

We sat in folding chairs near it. The flames were enormous, and the radiant heat from the fire pulsed against our faces and bodies in the starry night.

One of the persons in charge talked to us for a while about how to think about what is possible in our lives, what we wanted for ourselves. The other person patrolled the fire with a water hose to keep it in check. I was divided as to whether to give my attention to all the positive things being said or to worry about the fire containment.

We sat out under the stars for a long time as the fire burned down to a bed of molten coals. One man took a rake and began to rake the coals into a burning path. Then, we stood in a circle around the fire, contemplating what it might be like to put our bare feet on those burning coals, thousands of degrees of heat.

It began to happen. One by one, people began to take off their shoes and walk across the coals. As I watched them do it, I was rising inside, starting to see that my life really is just an idea in my head. "Think of your goal, and see it on the other side," the leader said. "Cross over to it."

I was willing. I took off my shoes and stepped out onto the burning coals in my bare feet. I began to walk and found that the coals felt soft, like walking on soft cotton. It did not even feel hot. I crossed and found myself delirious with joy. We all did it again, this time dancing in our bare feet in the fire under the night sky. It was incredible. It was real. Mind over matter. I could not sleep that night from the joy.

Step 1   Small Habit Changes

I suggest you start slowly and get used to the idea. Let's begin by changing patterns. Here are some easy ways to get started.

Change:

- The hand you use to hold your phone in when you are talking. If you usually hold it with your right hand, start holding it with your left hand.
- The side of the bed you sleep on. Move to the other side.
- The leg of your pants that you put on first when dressing.
- The way you drive home. Pick a different street to use to drive home.
- The kind of food you eat. Try some new things.

And so on...   What other patterns can you change?

Step 2. Small Risks

Once you have gotten used to making some small habit changes, consider taking some small risks that do not harm you but move you outside of your comfort zone. Here are some ideas of small risks, and perhaps you can create some others that are distinctive to your own special areas of fear. As you get accustomed to these small risks, you begin to build new muscles of courage to support you in your new life.

Small risks

- Give $5 to a stranger on the street.
- Ask the person behind you in line if they have the extra pennies you need to complete your purchase.
- Call someone you are upset with and tell him or her that you forgive him or her.

- When an argument begins with someone, tell that person that he or she is right and you are wrong, even if you are not sure you understand their point of view. Risk seeing it their way.
- Speak up about your opinion in a public meeting, or write a letter to an official, giving your view.
- Do something really nice for someone you don't like.
- Ask a favor of a neighbor you don't know well.
- Do a favor for a neighbor you don't know well.
- Sign up to learn a new sport that you know nothing about.
- Take a class in singing or public speaking.

And so on. Take some small risks that make you stretch. And when you do this, keep your intention in mind. These little daily situations mean very little compared to your intention to grow and expand your consciousness of wealth. These are all little stepping stones to help you do it.

Step 3   Revise your Dreams

Are you willing to stretch in your dreams? Revisit the first chapters of this workbook and see where you were in your intentions then. Could these be bigger, broader, more colorful, more successful? Give some thought to what you are creating in your life. Take a risk in your thinking. Take a quantum leap in your life. Jump. What would you attempt if you knew you could not fail? What would you dream if you knew it would all come true? Let's move into the miracle of all that is possible for you.

The Life of the Soul

It is important to have some perspective on your own spiritual journey and how it unfolds. The inner life is different than the outer life, and it is confusing to impose the values of one upon the other. Motivations we have for ourselves in the outer world are different than the values we hold true in the inner world.

In the outer world, we are motivated to be happy, to be prosperous, to be loved, to be healthy, to be useful and creative in our work, and to lead long, joyful lives. Because of the way that our material world works, our days can fill up with influences from media, advertising, opportunities, and advice from other people on how to create this kind of life for ourselves.

If we know someone who has been very successful in real estate, for example, we may think about getting into real estate ourselves, modeling ourselves after what seems to work for others. If friends of ours have lots of children and seem happy, we may decide that we need to have children to be happy. All of this sort of guess work, looking at the outside to create happiness on the inside, is the path of trial and error: the path of pain. It may seem to work for awhile, but then, inevitably, things start to fall apart. Life gets challenging, and at some point (if we are lucky), we are forced to turn within and choose again. We ask ourselves the hard questions: What really makes me happy? What is my real purpose for my life? Who do I think I really am —a mortal man or an eternal spirit?

In the inner world, we are motivated by truth, love, and joy. When we take our power back from the outer world and place it where it belongs, at the center of our hearts, all the answers become clear. Meditation is one doorway to this kind of inner dialogue.

This is the life of the soul, of your own individual spirit, and it has its own ways. Your soul would rather speak the truth, no matter what the cost, than hide in falsehood. Your soul would rather love all people, no matter what they do, than judge them, punish them, or get angry. Your soul would rather express every talent it has than make all the money in the world. Your soul would rather lead a short, delicious, passionate, joyful life with people you love, than live forever with those that you don't. And the great miracle is: when you give your soul, your infinite spirit, permission to decide how you live, your life begins to work and be joyous. Have you tried it? Can you do it every day?

Look from the inside. Each and every situation and person in your life is there to encourage you along the path of your own spirit. Ask the questions: How am I more joyful, more truthful, more loving, more creative because of this? How *could* I be more joyful because of this? What is my inner being expressing because I am having this experience?

Your spirit is seeking and finding ways to express its truth in every moment. When you do not align with it, you experience resistance, suffering, and pain. When you align with the power of your own spirit expressing itself, your life reflects truth and joy; you realize who you are and why you are here. This is how life works and why life is the way it is.

Today I kneel to only truth. Follow only beauty. Obey only love.

Kahlil Gibran

Game for a New Perspective

This little game will give you an opportunity to play with the perspectives you hold for your life. To achieve the greatest benefit, approach it with curiosity and a light heart.

Creating the Cards

You will need five or more 3x5 inch cards.

Write one card at a time.

On one side of the card, write a difficult situation you are having with your money right now.

On the other side, write the spiritual truth of you.

Example:

Side 1: I don't have money to do the things I want to do.

Side 2: I am a spiritual being, completely unconstrained by material things. I am free.

Write these kinds of things on each of your cards. Write the human problem on the first side of the card and the spiritual truth on the flip side of the card. Make five cards.

How to Play

Now, sit down quietly and center yourself.

Read side one of the first card, then read side two.

Go back and read side one, and then side two.

Keep flipping the card over and over, reading both sides. Do this with one card at a time, flipping back and forth, until you start to feel the situation release.

Move on to the next card and do the same.

Repeat with all of your cards, until you feel each situation start to release in your feelings about it.

Put the card away and do it again in a few hours, or the next day.

Continue to do this, flipping the cards side to side each day until you find the emotions or fears attached to each situation are gone, or at least very diminished.

What happened? It makes no logical sense to the mind. But your inner self came forward and brought the truth to these situations.

Don't try to analyze it. Just open and receive the release and freedom of your own essence and truth. *When you are complete with these cards, make some more. Use this as a game to help you change your life.*

How does it work?

Your heart knows the truth when it hears it. This little game is one way to draw out the truth of a situation and take power back from the outer world. It starts to reduce the attachment you have to your problems so that you can let them go.

This is an energetic exercise, and it does not have to be logical to work. Energy exercises are very powerful and work with the dynamic of the situation to shift it. Just notice how you feel before and after doing it.

The Experience of Opposites

Our entire life is an experience of opposites. Beginning with the most essential experiences: every day we experience hours of light when the sun is in our sky, and hours of darkness when the rotation of the earth blocks the sun from view. Every day we are awake for certain hours and asleep for certain hours. Every day we breathe air in and then we breathe air out.

Looking deeper, we find these opposites in everything we do and feel. Sometimes we feel we are completely right about something. Other times we feel we are wrong. Sometimes we are very interested in what is going on around us. Other times we have no interest. Sometimes we love the people we are with. Other times, we don't. And so the pendulum of life continues to swing in all that we do. Forward and backward. Up and down. In and out. So it goes. The great march of opposites makes up our daily lives.

From a financial point of view, this can be particularly painful. Sometimes we have money and sometimes we don't. The interesting thing about money is that we take it so personally. We use it to measure ourselves, to judge ourselves, to define ourselves. We may have lots of history with this idea. Our parents, our families, our friends may do this as well. Perhaps from a very early age, our personal value may have been judged by the state of our finances. As Woody Allen said: *"Money is better than poverty, if only for financial reasons."*

From the spiritual point of view, there is no truth to any of this. Being at one end of the pendulum swing of life, whether it be with money or love or time or health, being at the extremes of any of these, either high or low, does not in any way make you a better or worse person. Your value is not measured by your situation. You are a divine spirit with an unconditional nature, unaffected by external things. Your human condition, whether you are sick or well, rich or poor, does not change who you really are at all.

It is important to try to achieve some mastery of the full range of opposites in your life. Here is how you do it:

1. Recognize that human life contains opposites in everything. If you look hard enough, you can find examples in every area of opposites at work in our world.

2. Realize that human values attached to these opposites are just that: human values. They are just worldly ideas and are not the truth. You can decide to love yourself if you are fat or thin. You are still the same person. But many people decide they have no value if they gain weight. They are attaching to one side of the pole of opposites.

3. Realize that you are the same pure spirit no matter where you are on the pole of opposites in everything in your life. No matter what you are experiencing in your life, it is just that: an experience. It does not define you or make you any less or more than you already are. You are equally important if you are rich or poor.

4. You can achieve mastery of your experience of opposites by practice. Life has a way of giving us this kind of practice, whether we are ready for it or not. But you can grow greatly in your personal power and mastery by creating ways to practice this dynamic for yourself.

The next exercise gives you a chance to practice with opposites.

Working with Opposites

On these poles of opposites below, mark where you are now.

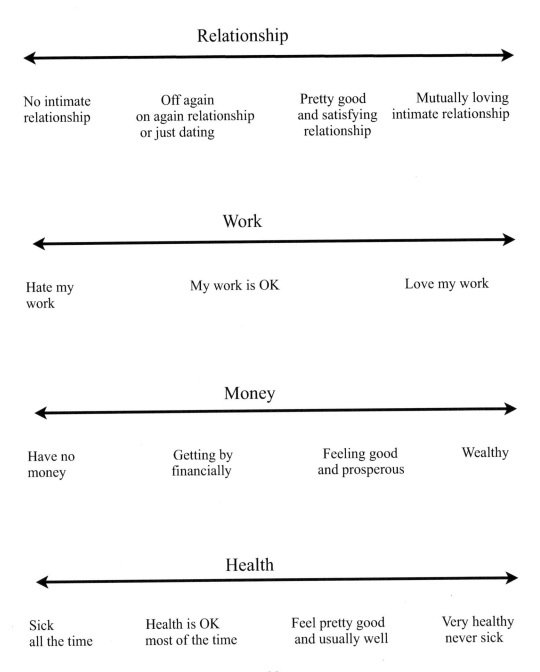

Relationship

No intimate
relationship

Off again
on again relationship
or just dating

Pretty good
and satisfying
relationship

Mutually loving
intimate relationship

Work

Hate my
work

My work is OK

Love my work

Money

Have no
money

Getting by
financially

Feeling good
and prosperous

Wealthy

Health

Sick
all the time

Health is OK
most of the time

Feel pretty good
and usually well

Very healthy
never sick

Now go back over the poles, and mark every point on the pole where you have been so far in your life. Mark EVERY point on the line that has been a place you have experienced in your life.

Now look at your marks. What do you see?

One student's pole of relationships looks like this: a picture of all the experiences she has had:

| No intimate relationship | Off again on again relationship or just dating | Pretty good and satisfying relationship | Mutually loving relationship |

So what does it mean? Well, taking a look at all the points she has experienced (and there are probably more than this), you can see that she has had experience at both extremes and quite a few in between. This is the pole of opposites of romantic love, and she has had experience at many different levels.

Do any of these define her or make her any less valuable than she is? No. Do these experiences teach her various things and give her the opportunity for spiritual insight? Definitely. She has had the experience of loving deeply another human being, and this presented her the opportunity to express her deeply loving nature. She had the opportunity to have pretty good relationships that tested her spiritually, since the soul impulse is to love deeply. But, by spending time on this moderating point on the scale of love, she has learned how to balance her patience and appreciation for another with her understanding of herself. When she was alone, she had a different set of insights. Perhaps this time, being alone allowed her to spend more time learning or having an experience that she could only have alone.

The important point here is that these are only experiences and do not in any way diminish her as a person or as a spiritual being. She has moved up and down the range of opposites in love during her human life in order to give herself the opportunities for understanding love on all levels. This has been part of her spiritual path.

With all of this in mind, let's turn to the pole of opposites in money. How does yours look? Have you had the opportunity to experience various levels of prosperity in your life? If so, you have had the chance to examine from many different angles what it means to be prosperous and how money can work in your life. This is great for understanding yourself, although it may be challenging for your human life. Our world is so materialistic that it can be less forgiving about money than other things.

Even so, you can regain your power over how this all plays out in your life. These can be conscious decisions, and by being conscious, you are completely free to choose which levels you create for your money. Let's take a closer look.

Here is a student's pole of opposites regarding money.

| Has no money | Getting by financially | Feeling good and prosperous | Wealthy |

Once again, we see that she has had an experience of opposites. This is encouraging from a spiritual point of view because it indicates that her brave soul is willing to experiment in experiencing differing levels of financial prosperity in her life. Once again, did any of these levels make her any less of a spiritual being? Do they make you any less of a spiritual being? This is an important concept. Once you see clearly that your money, or lack of money, does not define you or diminish your true self, then you are free to take back your control over the levels at which you live.

There are several ways to do this:

1. Mental Change Exercise

Write down a complete description of your current financial situation. Write every detail of it, from your bank balances to your bills to your current money supply. Get it all down on paper. When you feel it is complete, hold that complete description in your hand. Ask yourself: is this really who I am?

<u>On a new sheet of paper</u>, make a list of all the insights you are receiving because of the current level of your finances.

a. Name what you have learned about yourself because of this experience of money. Name the good things and the things you don't like so much. Name them and accept them as where you are right now. When you can be open to accepting where you are now, you are ready to let it go and change.

b. How do you understand your own spirit more because of it? Are you more or less patient, loving, fearful, creative because of this situation? When you have gained the spiritual insight from the situation, you no longer need to be at that level. You have found what your spirit wanted you to know, so you are ready for a new experience. Contemplate your new findings.

c. What insights will you find from being wealthy? Everyone has a different idea of what being wealthy would bring to their life. What will it bring to yours? Will you understand yourself more clearly when you are wealthy? What will it teach you about yourself that you don't know now?

d. Most importantly, how will you contribute to the universal good of all life by being wealthy?

Write down all of your answers.

Embodiment

Take hold of the information you receive—the insights, understandings, findings on all levels, all that you are learning—and try to fully embody them. Breathe these new insights into your body and try to give yourself a physical experience of them. Say to yourself that this is how I feel when I am experiencing these ideas. For example, "I feel the compassion or the patience or the joy. I know this, understand this, completely feel this experience until I am complete with it". Continue to give yourself this experience until you feel complete.

When you can embody these experiences, you no longer need to live at them out through pain and suffering. You can release the outer experience that brought them to you. Tear up the picture of your finances and throw it away.

Contemplate the list of your new insights and the new gifts you bring back from this experience. Be grateful for them. You are on your way to financial freedom

Example:

Wendy had always wanted to be financially independent but found instead that she was always dependent upon others. She created a very poor situation where a boyfriend she no longer even liked was paying her bills for her and so occupying her time that she did not have time to work. It seemed a vicious circle: she needed him to pay her bills, and the more he did, the more time he wanted from her. She was financially OK, but it all rested upon him, which gave her the experience of being penniless and dependent in ways that she hated.

By working with the idea of opposites, she began to understand that not having money was only an experience on the scale of opposites. It was the result of choices she had made. By changing her thinking, she could move to the opposite end of the pole. Money was not a measure of her true value. She began to think of herself as a powerful, valuable person having an experience on the pole of opposites. She could choose differently.

In her long evenings at home, she began to turn her creativity to learning how to design blogs and websites online. After much trial and error, she found that she enjoyed it and was good at it. She decided to set up her own website for her services as a designer.

Several of her friends saw her work and asked her to help them with their websites. This led to more people inquiring for help. Eventually, Wendy gained a strong clientele who paid her well. Soon, she was able to support herself and end her dysfunctional relationship. Her creativity and appreciation for her own talents caused her to blossom into productivity and joy in the outer world. Her finances began to reflect her new, more empowered way of thinking. Soon she was self-sufficient and financially free.

2. Emotional Change Exercise

How are you feeling about your money situation? Are you fearful? Are you angry or resentful? Do you blame someone else for your situation? Do you blame the economy or the banks or the company you work for or your boss? Do you blame yourself? Are you disappointed, depressed, worried? How do you feel?

One thing we know about life and how it works is that even feelings take place for a spiritual purpose. Whatever you are feeling is all part of the spiritual journey you are on. At some deep level, these emotions are designed to prompt you into action or to open you to a deeper understanding of yourself. So, let's use them now, consciously, to support you in consciously choosing the levels of prosperity you desire.

Find a quiet place to sit undisturbed. Remember that you are a spirit, living in this human world. You are here powerfully creating your life in this body. Your full attention is the full attention of the divine spirit you are.

So, turn your attention now to your feelings about your financial situation. Try to be as authentic as possible and truly feel the negative emotions you have. Choose one emotion to concentrate on for this exercise, perhaps fear, for example.

Bring your full attention to your fear. Fill up your mind with it. Think of nothing else but your fear. Hold that fear in your mind and just feel the fear as hard as you can. Fill up your mind completely with fear and hold it there. See if you can hold this for 5 minutes.

Notice that an interesting thing starts to happen. Because you are a very powerful spirit, if you do this long enough, the fear will begin to diminish. Your attention will begin to dissolve the fear. There is an important spiritual lesson here: the light always dispels the darkness. Even when it does not seem that way in our lives, it is true that anything that is not life giving will eventually die. Life favors all that creates more life.

This powerful principle is at work in this exercise. The light of your attention dissolves the darkness of your fear. It may take some time but it will. Don't take my word for it, do the exercise for yourself. See and feel your fear dissolve. If this takes a few times to be completely gone, OK. Be strong and hold your attention firmly until it dissolves.

The profound truth of this exercise is very important for you to understand. When you turn your spiritual power fully in the direction of your human emotions, any false ideas and feelings give way and dissolve as you hold them in the presence of your spiritual truth.

Keep trying this exercise until it becomes easy for you. Remember that the attention of your spirit in its full focus will dissolve anything negative or unlike itself. Take your worst ideas and emotions and dissolve them in the light of your truth.

3. Spiritual Change Exercise

The most transformative way to work with opposites is to use them as spiritual symbols of your own growth and progress.

To demonstrate: turn within once again and see where you are on your scale of prosperity opposites. Are you feeling broke? Wealthy? Barely getting by? Feel where you are.

Ask yourself deeply, what is the purpose of this experience on the pole of opposites? Am I discovering how to be patient? Am I learning compassion? Am I learning to have faith in myself and in how life works? Am I being pushed to create and express my talents in a whole new way? There are so many answers possible. Look for the answer that encourages you the most, in your understanding of how your life is working.

Whatever the purpose is, breath it into your heart. Imagine that you are taking this idea inside of your body and feeling this purpose physically. Hold this spiritual purpose within you and feel how it feels to fully experience it. Be grateful for it and for the greater expansion it is bringing to you. Realize that it is an important part of your life, to have this experience. Take your time. Truly feel this experience within your whole being.

And then let it go. Release it back to life. Breathe it out of your body in one great breath. With gratitude let it go. And then, when it is completely released, check in again on your scale of opposites and see that you have moved to a new place. Speak a word of gratitude and joy. Practice with this powerful tool until it becomes easy for you.

Projection and Personalization

The wisest discovery that psychology has ever made is this: all you see happening in life is a projection of your own past experiences, issues and beliefs. It is as if you are looking through a lens, colored by your own ideas and emotions which filters out everything that contradicts either how you see yourself or how you see the world. It reflects your own beliefs back to you.

If you want to see what you think, take a hard look at the people around you. They are playing it all out for you to see clearly. Everything you judge and criticize them for is a projection of what you criticize about yourself. And this is also true of them. They see you through their own lens, which projects their past experiences, feelings and beliefs onto you.

This understanding serves you in two big ways. On one hand, just looking at the people in your life reflects what is going on inside of you. This is a gift to you, since seeing ourselves clearly is one of the hardest things to do.

On the other hand, when someone else criticizes you, or argues with you or does something that hurts your feelings, you do not need to take it personally. Like you, all they can see are their own issues. So whatever they are dishing out to you is about them, not about you. Don't take it personally.

These two ideas: projection and personalization, remind us that life is not what it seems on the outside. Truth is always found on the inside. Only found on the inside. Always.

So, you might ask," Why did my parents mistreat me? I was so little, this could not be my choice." No, it was theirs. They were projecting their own issues onto you and taking it out on you. Because you were little, and did not understand, you took it personally. It was always about them, not about you. This does not make it right or desirable. But it does explain why it happened the way it did.

This is a big topic and we could spend a lot of time sorting through everything that has happened in your life, everything that has happened in our world, to see these concepts at work. But, for the purposes of this book, let's apply these ideas to money. Because each life is so unique, it is easier to understand when we look at the detailed point of view.

Symbols of money exercise

Create a statement about how you see someone else handling his or her money and write it in the first column. In the second column, write how it reflects you and your life.

Example:

What I See	How It Reflects Me
I think the government should free up more bank loans and more assistance to help the economy. They don't spend the time to figure out how to free up more money. We are all suffering because of it.	I wish I had more money to spend to have a better lifestyle. I am not doing enough to make it happen and to help myself be prosperous There are ways I could free up my money but I'm not doing it.

Create five statements and reflections like the ones in the example and write them in the appropriate columns like the example below.

If you have trouble finding the reflection, cross out the "She" or "He" or "They" in the first statement and substitute "I" in the second statement.

What I See	How It Reflects Me

How to Use Your Reflection

This list of how your world reflects you is one of the most powerful tools you have for expanding your prosperity. If you are critical of others and of yourself, you are placing that idea in the unified field and attracting more occasions for criticism. If you are judgmental of others and of yourself, you are pushing your own natural good away from you. If you see suffering, hardship, war, despair around you, it is also within you. So this is a very useful tool for discovering any issues that are blocking or diminishing your prosperity. As you uncover them, go back to chapter 3 and use one or more of the exercises for clearing them.

Please don't feel, however, that you have to change everything about yourself to move into the consciousness of wealth. The spiritual process of changing is very forgiving and easier than you think. In the next chapter, you will find all of these ideas coming together.

Seeds of Consciousness

ideas to plant within your mind

1. As I am willing to take small risks and make changes on the outside, I am able to expand on the inside. This supports me in changing my life. I am open to change.

2. My true self is my Spirit. I am unbounded and free.

3. Life is filled with opposite ways of living. I am strong and powerful and can live at any of these opposite stages without it changing who I am as a powerful spiritual being.

4. My life reflects back to me all the ideas, feelings, and thoughts I am holding inside. By noticing what I see around me, I can see the reflection of myself. I can use this reflection to find my way to greater prosperity.

Nighttime Journal

Before bed, journal each night about the following questions. Use any of the exercises from this chapter to clear anything that comes up during this activity.

Where was my experience on the pole of opposites of prosperity today?

How did this reflect my beliefs? What am I willing to believe tomorrow?

Who supported me today?

Who did I give to today?

What am I most grateful for today?

8. THE WISDOM WITHIN

I once took a workshop where the homework assignment was to get ten gifts and give them to ten strangers. Have you ever done anything like this? Because I can be shy about approaching strangers, this was challenging to me. I decided to get ten fairly good looking pens at a nearby discount store. And then I would go to a local shopping mall and give them away.

Tentatively, I approached the first person and held out one pen. "This seems like a nice pen", I said. "Would you like it?" To my surprise, he did, saying "Thank you," and walked away with it. It gave me the courage to approach another person. She also liked it and took it.

And then something very powerful started to happen. As I walked through the shopping center, I began to be able to spot the particular stranger who would like the pen. And even more surprising, they began to spot me. As I entered a store, someone there would turn around and look at me and wait for me to approach them to give them the pen. I knew exactly who to ask each time. It was as if, in some inner realm, there was an understanding between us even before I walked into the store.

I began to feel that I especially liked these people. They saw me and knew me in some sort of way. And I knew them. This was all happening around many other people who were completely oblivious to what was going on. They just went about their shopping, not knowing me or even seeing me there in the store.

As this exercise continued, I entered into a new state that felt like an altered state of consciousness. I was beginning to feel the great web of connections between myself and those who were at a similar vibration as me. We understood each other. We saw each other. And I gave them a pen. I felt joyous and connected and inspired. I had the sense of being a part of a community of the heart, along with these other special individuals. We all, in some unspoken way, knew each other even though we had never met each other.

These feelings stayed with me afterward, on the way home, and for many days after. By giving gifts to the right strangers, I had found that I did not walk this earth alone. There was a community of like-minded souls who were walking with me. And even though I might not know where they are right now, I know they are there.

It is experiences such as this that open up our eyes to see the true nature of reality. Sometimes it happens with the birth of a baby, when that new soul bursts onto the human stage and we experience the pure miracle of life itself. Sometimes it happens with a death, when someone we love leaves their body behind and we have a true sense of how thin the line is between life and death. Sometimes a pure scarlet blossom takes our breath away, or the sheer beauty of the ocean overwhelms our senses so that we know for sure, in that moment, that there is so much more to life than meets the eye. Or we hear of someone's suffering on the news, a war, a deadly storm, a tragedy, and our heart opens up wide enough for the entire human race to take up home there. We realize the value of each beautiful soul on this planet, and then go home and hug our own loved ones with gratitude.

Our life, your life, is a miracle. The outer appearances are a very thin veneer over the powerful spiritual life at work in every moment. The life of the individual spirit, the inner path, underlies everything that takes place in the outer world. When we can practice seeing this, or train ourselves to interpret human events this way, we are standing on truth. The perfection of the inner way reveals itself. We are able to make sense of our lives and live with purpose and joy.

Symbols in My World

To truly go deeper into your own being, it is important to approach it with a pilgrim's mind: a mind that is clear, open and willing to learn. Can you let go of old ways for a moment and try on some different ideas? To consciously live as a spirit gives you the ability to experience your life in a completely new way. The beauty of it will delight you and the perfection of it will astonish you. Even more, the ability you already have to line up with your highest good and create your dreams will become so apparent to you that your life will be transformed. Once you see through to the truth of life, you can never go back to the old unconscious ways of living.

This is why money is such an excellent tool for your transformation. Because our culture puts such a superficial, materialistic meaning on money, it seems the farthest point from spiritual progress. But it is not. In some ways, it is the closest point because its message is so obvious and easy to understand.

Take a Day of Retreat

To better understand the deeper meanings of life, I recommend that you take a day (yes, one whole day) and use your time to transform your relationship with your money and your life.

Retreat is a doorway into the inner, symbolic world in which we all live. It is a way to strengthen your faith muscles and learn to see the truth of the spiritual universe. Do you have to do this day of retreat to experience a greater flow of wealth in your life? No, but it helps so much. Even if you decide not to do a full day of retreat, consider adding its practices to your daily life. The important thing is to stop your regular schedule and give yourself time for deeply considering all that we have discussed in this book, all the elements of your life and allow time to make new intentions for the future.

Come to this day well rested with the commitment to seriously do this work. Decide that the rest of your life can wait for one day to allow you to have this experience. Let your loved ones and those to whom you are responsible know that you are not reachable on this day. Turn off your phone. The night before your retreat, as you go to bed, spend a few quiet moments. Allow yourself to connect with that deep knowing within. Make a commitment to yourself to truly surrender to this day of retreat and all that it has to teach you.

You are preparing to create a new plan, a new pattern for your life. This new way of being will fulfill your dreams much more than the life you are living now. So, take time to review all that you have done so far with this book and all of your ideas, answers and journaling from its pages.

Items you will need for your day of retreat:

A peaceful space where you can be alone

No phones, TV, computers, or other distraction.

Some meditative music

A nice candle

A soft pillow and blanket

A journal for writing, and markers or crayons

Highly nutritious snacks to have throughout the day

Lots of fresh water

Access to nature or other place to walk

This book and the work you have done thus far

Elements to include in your retreat day:

Journaling

Gentle exercise

Meditation

Silence

Time in nature

Free time to do nothing but just be

Time to complete the exercises on the following pages

See how nature - trees, flowers, grass - grow in silence, see the stars, the moon and the sun, how they move in silence...we need silence to be able to touch our souls.

Mother Teresa

Wisdom of the Heart

Here is a wonderful exercise to include in your time of retreat, or to do thoughtfully in your quiet time. Take a piece of paper and draw lines on it to make three columns as you see below.

Person	Quality	Symbol

Make a list in the first column of every person you admire. These can be people you know or public figures, historical figures, anyone you admire.

In the second column, write the qualities they have that cause you to admire them. Are they brave, strong, loving, creative? Write their good qualities.

In the third column, decide what each person symbolizes for you. Just as we did with the sun and the natural world, decide the symbolic nature of those you admire in your life. Sometimes we have a person in our life who just oozes love. He or she simply *is* love for us. Or perhaps, you have another person in your life who is extremely smart. He or she *is* intelligence for you. That is his or her symbol in your life. Some people *are* love or intelligence or joy or other things. If you need support in deciding, go within and ask your heart its answer.

You can also imagine the face of the person in your mind and imagining you are looking through them or into them, find the symbol they have in your life. Sit with these ideas until you find the symbolic meaning that seems right to you.

Now go back and look at your list. Read down the list of qualities you have written. Pay attention to this list. These are also qualities of you. You could not recognize and value them in others if you did not already have them in yourself. They are reflecting your qualities back to you. Some of these qualities may be more developed in you than others. But they are all there.

Look at the symbols for each person. Everyone in your life shows up to assist you on your path. All are symbols of what you are needing or exploring in life. Yes, these people are real and have their own lives. But at a deeper level, in your mystical nature, they are symbols to your soul. They are there to assist you when you are seeking answers or wisdom for your own life.

Look and see. Who symbolizes peace? When you need peace, go to him or her. Who symbolizes creativity? When you need a new idea, ask him or her. Who symbolizes freedom? When you need these answers, ask him or her. Do you see how it works? Let your heart guide you. Find its truth within.

Questions for My Life

Now we can use these qualities and people to answer some of the deeper questions you may have.

Write 3 questions you have about your life.

1.

2.

3.

Now go back to your list of the people in your life and their symbols. Let each of these inner symbols offer answers to your questions. Try to work with the symbol, not the personality of the individual in your life.

Example:
Question: What can I do to have more money in my life?
Ask my symbols.

Here is an example. One woman put down on her list that Martha Stuart was a person she admired. The qualities she saw in her were attention to detail, elegance, and the ability to support herself doing what she loved. For this woman, Martha Stuart symbolized an expression of loving creativity.

So, how would that apply to the question of how to have more money in life? She had to ask herself: What would loving creativity tell me to do? After contemplating this question, she began to think of her great love of gardening. Every season she loved working in the soil and growing the most beautiful seasonal plants. How could she take this great love and use it creatively to have more money? After some time of journaling over this question, she decided to put her own love to work and share her knowledge with others. She started an online blog about seasonal gardening and began teach others how to choose and plant by season. This was an activity that she loved and, over time, she built a following and was able to charge a subscription for her newsletter of planting tips and resources. Soon more money began to flow into her life.

Now, try this for yourself. Spend some time with your list and begin to make notes of ways these qualities and symbols could help you answer the questions you have in your life.

Example:

What would freedom tell me to do? Freedom would tell me to arrange my daily schedule so that I am not so tired and have more energy to create new ways of earning in my life.

What would peace tell me to do? Peace would tell me to relax and to have more faith, to follow my heart and to know that my life is unfolding according to my intentions. Peace would teach me forgiveness and patience.

These are examples, but you will have your own answers. Start with your question number one .

Your Question 1

Ask yourself your question and then look at the symbols on your other list. Ask yourself what would peace say about this? What would freedom say? What would creativity say? Use the symbols you have created and let them offer their answers to your questions. Write down the answers.

Your Question 2

Ask yourself your question and then look at the symbols on your other list. Ask yourself, what would peace say about this? What would freedom say? What would creativity say? Use the symbols you have created and let them offer their answers to your questions. Write down the answers.

Your Question 3

Ask yourself your question and then look at the symbols on your other list. Ask yourself, what would peace say about this? What would freedom say? What would creativity say? Use the symbols you have created and let them offer their answers to your questions. Write down the answers.

If you followed these answers, how would your life change?

Journal about your answers and any other ideas that present themselves now.

Symbols of Money in My Life

Let's take all that we have done and add in the idea of money. What does money symbolize for you in your life? Is it more than one thing? For some it is love. For some it is freedom. For some it is peace and so on. Write what money symbolizes for you.

Now revisit each of your questions about your life.

Ask:

- What is my money saying to me about these questions?
- What guidance am I receiving through my money?
- How can I use this wisdom to move into a new level of wealth and well being?

My Dreams Coming True

As you discover these answers, what steps will you take to make your dreams come true? Go back over all that you have written as answers to your questions. These are the answers you have been looking for. Use them now to create an action plan for making your dreams come true.

1.   Make a list of the actions you will take starting today.

2.   What steps will you take for yourself?

3.   What steps will you take for your community?

4.   What steps will you take for the world?

Make a commitment to follow these steps to create a new way of life for yourself.

Seeds of Consciousness

ideas to plant within your mind

1. Everything in my life is here for my good. By going within and listening to my heart, I have all the answers necessary to find my way.

2. By paying attention to the life around me, I realize that this is truly a spiritual universe. I see the reflections of my inner self everywhere I look.

3. Money is one more opportunity to move into the direction of my dreams. I am willing to listen and to realize that I can make my dreams come true.

Nighttime Journal

Before bed, journal each night about the following questions.

Where on the pole of prosperity was my money situation today?

How did this reflect the symbols money holds for me?

What am I guided to do?

What do freedom and truth say about this?

What do creativity and joy say about this for me?

9. GRATEFUL TO RECEIVE

The great adventure of life continues on, but now you have new tools and a concrete list of steps to take to create a life of greater well being inside and out. By clearing all that has been blocking you, making a new commitment to your own truth and learning to interpret the activity of your money, you are powerfully able to create an exciting new level of prosperity and joy. Life continues to shift and change, so when you find yourself at a different point on the pole of opposites, revisit these exercises and make a new choice by listening to the wisdom of your money. In every moment, you hold the power to change the level of your wealth, working from the inside out. As you expand, your money will flow in ways that you once thought impossible. But now, it is just the way it all works.

No discussion of money would be complete without remembering gratitude. Once again, we are talking about spiritual gratitude. Human gratitude may be a kind way of thanking someone for something he or she did for you. Spiritual gratitude is different.

Spiritual gratitude is a way of life. In our spiritual nature, we celebrate deeply the opportunity of life and all that it offers. We celebrate our bountiful world and the amazing beauty and pleasure it offers. We celebrate ourselves, knowing that we are complex beings: spiritual and human at once. We live in a unified field of all life, and within it we are on the grand adventure of the individualized spirit in time and space in this world. There is so much to be grateful for.

But spiritual gratitude is even more than that, because true spiritual gratitude knows that our life is good at its essence, its core. We know that because of this, whatever is coming next is also good and for our highest benefit. And so, we are grateful before it even gets here. We are grateful all the time. Because of the way life works, this tremendous flow of gratitude moves into consciousness and creates more and more good to be grateful for in our lives. More reasons for gratitude.

So, today and every day, be grateful for your life, your wisdom, and your wealth. Let your overflow of gratitude move into the unified field and create a tremendous new vibration of wealth for you. You deserve it. It is yours by the nature of who you are. Be grateful to receive it and live it now.

Wealth and well-being are yours
by the nature of who you are.
Listen to your heart and the
Wisdom of your Money. Be who
you came here to be.

Alice Bandy

Join Dr. Alice Bandy in her online class

the Consciousness
of Wealth.

You are invited to go deeper with Dr. Alice Bandy by participating in her new online class, *The Consciousness of Wealth,* a groundbreaking new, self-study course that guides you to deeper levels of awareness, greater joy and helps you clear forever all of the old blocks to prosperity that you have in your life.

The Consciousness of Wealth offers you 8 weeks of lessons, activities, exercises and videos to further explain and support you in great wealth and well-being. Listen to 8 recorded meditations from Dr. Alice that guide you into deeper awareness and realization. Play the Game of Life, a creative new way to download your issues onto a game board, and use powerful tools to clear them forever. Join in our *Consciousness of Wealth* private Facebook page where you can chat with other students and ask your questions of Dr. Alice. Receive daily email inspiration, ideas and tools for 30 more days after you complete the course.

Here's what others who have taken this course have to say:
   "I removed blocks to my prosperity I did not even know had."
   "Marvelous!"
   "Fun, encouraging and thought provoking."
   "A rare and extraordinary way to clear your path to a consciousness of wealth from the inside out."

To find out more and to register for this great new course, go to www.consciousnessofwealth.com

Dr. Alice Bandy
is the Spiritual Director of The Heart of Teaching, Inc. a nonprofit educational organization. She has been leading transformative spiritual classes for adults since 1996. Dr. Alice has taught at many universities and is a favorite instructor at Holmes Institute School of Consciousness Studies. In 2012, Holmes Institute granted her an honorary Doctorate for her achievements in authoring, teaching and disseminating powerful spiritual courses throughout the United States. Her creative style of teaching offers students experiences of personal empowerment designed to reveal the inherent greatness within each individual. She lives in Encinitas, California.
Visit her online at www.consciousnessofwealth.com.